Traditional
Scottish
Songs &
Music

Katherine Campbell
& Ewan McVicar

Illustrated by
Finola Stack

Leckie & Leckie

Dr Katherine Campbell obtained her BA (musical studies) at the Royal Scottish Academy of Music and Drama (validated by the University of Glasgow), her PGCE from Moray House, Edinburgh, and her PhD in ethnomusicology from the University of Edinburgh. She has tutored and lectured in Scottish music for both the RSAMD and the University of Edinburgh's School of Scottish Studies, and undertaken research work on various aspects of Scottish music. She has a wide range of performance experience as a singer and cellist, including much live performance work throughout Scotland and various studio recordings. She has also delivered papers to conferences on aspects of Scottish music and received a number of musical awards and scholarships. Her output includes contributions to books and periodicals. She is currently an Arts and Humanities Research Board (AHRB) Research Fellow in the Creative and Performing Arts at the School of Scottish Studies.

Ewan McVicar wrote a song called *Talking Army Blues* which reached the Top Twenty in 1960, and more recently has written some twenty songs for Scotland's top children's show, *The Singing Kettle*. Another twenty of his songs in the traditional song genre have been recorded commercially. His various publications include a book on the songs, songwriters and singers of Glasgow, a teaching pack on Scottish whaling songs, two further books, numerous articles and reviews, and radio scripts. He was Writer in Residence for two years in the schools of Craigmillar, Edinburgh. He has run workshops, given performances and organised projects in well over one hundred Scottish schools in the fields of Scottish traditional song, songwriting, storytelling and other related areas. He has performed on and produced several commercial recordings and has extensive performing experience. He has an MSc in Research from the University of Edinburgh, gained for work on Scottish Children's Songs conducted at the School of Scottish Studies.

Published by Leckie & Leckie Ltd, 8 Whitehill Terrace, St Andrews
Scotland KY16 8RN
Tel: 01334 475656   Fax: 01334 477392
hq@leckieandleckie.co.uk   www.leckieandleckie.co.uk
Leckie & Leckie Ltd is an Investor in People Company.
® Leckie & Leckie is a registered trademark.

INVESTOR IN PEOPLE

MADE IN SCOTLAND
Printed by Inglis Allen, Kirkcaldy.
Page layout by Redgate Creative, Cupar.
Thread-sewn by Hunter and Foulis, Edinburgh.

ISBN 1-898890-28-5

A CIP record for this book is available from the British Library.

ACKNOWLEDGEMENT
The material on Gaelic song is based on articles written by Morag MacLeod, Senior Lecturer at the School of Scottish Studies, University of Edinburgh, whose speciality is Gaelic song and who also transcribed and translated the Gaelic song lyrics.

MANY THANKS TO
Morag MacLeod of the School of Scottish Studies for advice and assistance. Dr Margaret Mackay, Director of the School of Scottish Studies, for advice and for permission to use material from the School's sound archive, issued on the 'Scottish Tradition' series by Greentrax. Ian D Green of Greentrax for advice and for permission to use Scottish Tradition material and other Greentrax recordings. Julia Lane of Castlebay for permission to use her clarsach track *The Lea Rig*. Josh Dickson for playing pipe and advising on our section about piping. Colin Campbell for playing fiddle. Mary Kennedy for playing accordion. Carol McMillan John Montgomery and David Nicoll.

Christine Kydd, traditional singer and Music Development Officer with the Tolbooth Project, Stirling, for her assistance. Liz Reid Music Specialist in Primary Schools, West Lothian, for advice. Dr Emily Lyle of the School of Scottish Studies for her interest and encouragement. Linda McVicar for proofreading the text.

George Haig of Pickled Egg Audio, Dunfermline for co-producing, recording and mastering the CD.

CONTENTS

INTRODUCTION

This book and CD give an introduction to the riches of traditional Scottish song and music. Popular songs usually talk about feelings but have little narrative. Traditional songs nearly always contain a story, and there are often other interesting stories associated with the songs. We have included some of these stories and versions of other old Scottish stories.

The book and CD are for use by anyone with an interest in Scottish traditional culture, including enthusiasts, students, teachers and musicians. We include sections exploring such terms as waulking song, Gaelic psalm, mouth music (puirt a beul), bothy ballad, strathspey, Scots ballad, pibroch, clarsach and Jacobite song.

The book has been structured so the material gradually becomes more complex. Primary school class and music teachers will find the material addresses relevant sections of the 5–14 Curriculum. Secondary school music teachers and Standard Grade students will find the material covers the Scottish components of the curriculum in a full and relevant way. Traditional musicians working in schools, with community groups or with individual students will find useful material on Scotland's musical traditions in this book.

TRADITIONAL

'Traditional' means that we do not know who wrote or composed a piece of music. The term is also sometimes applied to songs or tunes that are thought to be old, or have been so changed and amended over the years that they differ significantly from the original maker's work. That is why you may find in a book or on a recording a different version of a song or tune in this book. You may already know a piece but not agree with the lyrics or the tune that we give for it. However, it is not a case of right or wrong – the traditional process of oral learning means that several 'right' versions of a piece may exist.

Similarly, we do not give full transcriptions of the music on the CD, but have given a basic notation of the tune and accompanying chords that can be used. Players will apply their own interpretations to pieces, changing chords and adding 'grace notes'.

The 'traditional' label is also applied to some songs or tunes which are still performed very much as their makers created them, but are felt to be part of our common Scottish heritage and might well be called 'national' rather than 'traditional'. Examples of this are songs like *Flower of Scotland* and *I Belong To Glasgow*, tunes like *The Bonny Lass of Bon Accord*, and certain of the songs of Robert Burns and Harry Lauder.

NEW WORDS FOR OLD TUNES

When Burns put his own words to tunes that he already knew, he was following an old Scottish custom that songwriters still follow today. Some of our tunes have had many different sets of words put to them. A dance tune can be slowed right down to become a dramatic ballad, a noble old war tune can survive as a children's song, and singers can take the words of one song and the tune of another to create a new work.

TRADITIONAL STORIES

As well as the stories of songs and tunes, we have included some retold traditional and new Scottish stories. Some, such as *The Seal Wife*, are very old. Some, such as *The Well At The World's End* and *Giant Fitba,* are probably not true. Some, such as *The Loch of the Sword* and *David Down The Pit*, we think or know are true. Some, such as *The Worser*, might be true.

THE MUSIC AND THE CD

Most, but not all, of the songs and tunes in this book are included on the CD. Except where the CD performances are drawn from other recordings or consist of piping, the performance key is the same on the CD and in the book. We have included 'karaoke' mixes of five of the songs, with vocal tracks removed, for use as 'singalong' tracks in school.

Because individual interpretation and variation is the hallmark of traditional music and song, we give a basic notation of each melody which must be fitted flexibly to the lyrics in performance. We have also tried to give a clear and easy version of the chords that can accompany the songs and tunes in this book. Sometimes the chords on the CD will differ from those in the book.

Traditional Scottish Songs

Coulter's Candy

Track 1

This is now the best-known Scottish children's song. Some people use it as a lullaby, but it started as an advertising jingle.

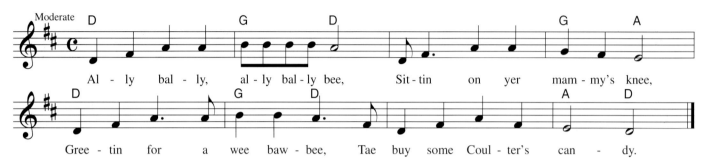

1) Ally bally, ally bally bee,
Sittin on yer mammy's knee,
Greetin for a wee bawbee,
Tae buy some Coulter's candy.

2) Willie wept baith lang and sair,
Till he got a penny tae share.
Noo he's tumblin doon the stair
Tae buy some Coulter's candy.

3) Poor wee Annie was greetin tae.
What could poor auld Mammy dae?
But gie them a penny atween them twae
Tae buy mair Coulter's candy.

4) Oor wee Jeannie wis lookin affa thin,
A rickle o banes covered ower wi skin.
Noo she's gettin a wee double chin,
Sookin Coulter's candy.

5) Here comes Coulter doon the street,
The man the bairns aa like tae meet,
His big black bag it hauds a treat,
It's full o Coulter's candy.

In the 1870s, Robert Coultart (that is how he spelt his name), a mill worker in Galashiels, made aniseed-flavoured hard toffee in his house and sold it around all the fairs and markets in the Borders. He played his whistle and made up this song to call the children to buy his sweets.

There are many old and new verses to the song. One of them says he wore a 'big lum hat', another that he carried a basket on his head. But a man called John A Anderson who saw him wrote, 'He wore a Tam o Shanter, or was it a Balmoral bonnet? With a pheasant's feather sticking straight up from a buckle above his ear. A shiny black bag slung over his shoulder held a stock of the famous candy!'

Some Scottish Songs for Singing to Small Children

Baloo Ba Leerie (a lullaby)

To get a baby to go to sleep.

Ba - loo ba lee - rie, Ba - loo ba lee - rie, Ba - loo ba lee - rie, Ba - loo ba - loo.

Dance Tae Yer Mazzie (a dandling song)

For bouncing a baby on your knee. There is a very well-known version of this song from Newcastle in north England, but here is one of the Scots versions.

Dance tae yer maz - zie, ma bon - ny las - sie, Dance tae yer maz - zie, ma bon - ny doo.

1) Dance tae yer mazzie, ma bonny lassie,
Dance tae yer mazzie, ma bonny doo.

2) Ye'll get a fishie, my bonny missie,
Ye'll get a fishie when the boats come in.

Clap Yer Handies (a clapping song)

To get a baby to clap its hands.

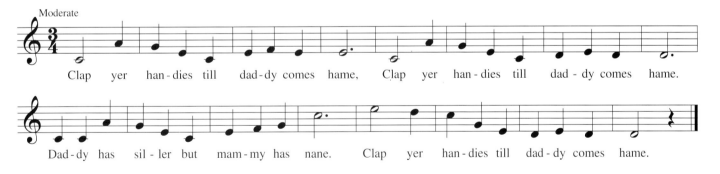

Clap yer han - dies till dad - dy comes hame, Clap yer han - dies till dad - dy comes hame.

Dad - dy has sil - ler but mam - my has nane. Clap yer han - dies till dad - dy comes hame.

Bee Baw Babbity

A very old song, used to amuse children or for a dance game.

Bee baw bab - bi - ty, Bab - bi - ty, bab - bi - ty. Bee baw bab - bi - ty, A las - sie or a wee lad - die?

1) Bee baw babbity,
Babbity, babbity.
Bee baw babbity,
A lassie or a wee laddie?

2) Choose, choose who you'll tak,
Who you'll tak, who you'll tak.
Choose, choose who you'll tak,
A lassie or a wee laddie?

Street Songs

Tracks 2 & 3

Some people call the short songs that Scottish children sing when they are playing 'street songs', but these days they are sung in the playground more than in the street.

Songs that used to be sung for ball bouncing, skipping or Chinese Ropes are now mostly used for hand-clapping.

Today is Hogmanay

Most songs that Scottish children sing are quite short and many of them are funny. This song is at least eighty years old. When you come to the 'ah ah ahs', hold your nose and gently tap yourself on the throat with the side of your other hand to imitate the sound of the bagpipes.

One Two Three Aleerie

Aleerie is a very old word that means holding your leg crooked. You would bounce the ball three times, then lift your leg and bounce the ball under it when you came to 'aleerie'. The song was also used for skipping and it has lots of other verses from different parts of Scotland.

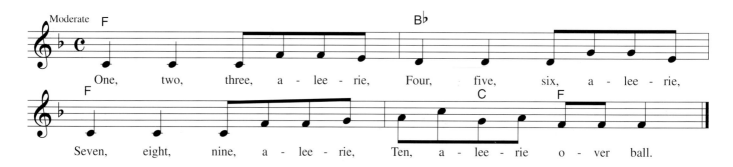

Wee Gallus Bloke

A city song about confident girls coming out from their factory. They meet a lad, and tell him what they think of him.

Track 4
Karaoke Track
33

1) As I came by the sweetie works, ma hairt began tae beat,
Seein aa the factory lassies comin doon the street,
Wi their flashy, dashy petticoats, flashy dashy shawls,
Five and a tanner gutty boots, 'Oh we're big gallus molls.'

2) As I came by the dancin, I began tae think.
Will aa the lassies stand an talk aboot oor Jeannie's mink?
Or will they hae a natter wi me aboot ma past?
But just as I came up tae them they walked away right fast.

CHORUS
Oh, yer ma wee gallus bloke nae mair.
Oh, yer ma wee gallus bloke nae mair.
Wi yer bell blue strides, yer bunnet tae the side,
Yer ma wee gallus bloke nae mair.

This song is full of words that somebody living in a Scottish city eighty years ago would have understood, but which now need to be explained. The 'sweetie works' is a sweet factory. Petticoats and shawls are clothing, 'gutty boots' are rubber boots like wellington boots (gutta-percha is a kind of rubber) and 'strides' are trousers. 'Five and a tanner' is five shillings and sixpence, or $27\frac{1}{2}$ pence – not much to pay for a pair of wellington boots these days! 'Gallus molls' is hard to translate from Glesga (Glasgow speech) into English. It means girls who are proud of themselves and their style.

The World Must Be Coming To An End

Track 5

A girl is sent to buy the 'messages' (groceries) in a shop, but she always meets with problems and often with catastrophe.

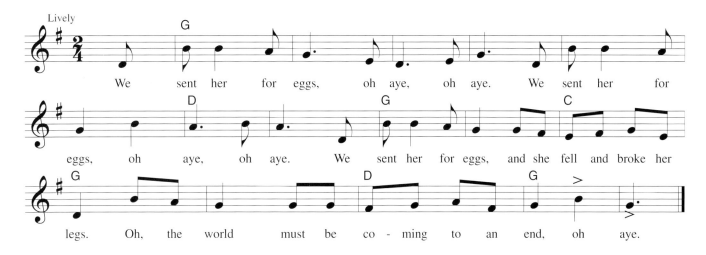

1) We sent her for eggs, oh aye, oh aye.
We sent her for eggs, oh aye, oh aye.
We sent her for eggs, and she fell and broke her legs.
Oh, the world must be coming to an end, oh aye.

2) We sent her for cheese, and she fell and skint her knees.

3) We sent her for butter, and she dropped it in the gutter.

4) We sent her for spaghetti, she got eaten by a Yeti.

5) We sent her for breid and she drapped doon deid.

When singing this song with younger children, they can form the letter 'O' with forefinger and thumb, and the letter 'I' with forefinger, each time 'oh' and 'aye' are sung.

The pronunciation can be made more Scottish or less so – you choose!

Scottish songwriters working in schools often use this song to show pupils how to begin songwriting. Here are just a few of the new verses that have been made by children.

We sent her for honey, she forgot to take the money.

We sent her for breid, and she fell and split her heid.

We sent her for bacon, and her poor wee legs were achin.

We sent her for jam and she brought back ham.

We sent her for a bun, and she came back as a nun.

We sent her for toothpaste, and she fell over a loose lace.

We sent her for a biscuit, but she didny want tae risk it.

We sent her for toast, and she came back loast.

She tried to cross the road, and she turned into a toad.

We sent her for mince, and we haven't seen her since.

The Well at the World's End

There was a girl whose mother sent her to the Well at the World's End to fetch some water to bake scones. But the well was dry. The girl sat down and cried.

Out popped a little green frog who said, 'Dinna cry, lass. If ye promise tae marry me ah'll get ye the water.'

The girl laughed and said, 'All right, ah'll marry you.'

The frog jumped into the bushes and began to dig. Water came rushing into the well, and the girl filled her jug and ran off home without saying 'Thank you.'

That night there came a sound at the girl's door. A little voice was singing, 'Open the door, ma promised wife, open the door, ma honey, ma dear.'

The girl's mother said, 'Who's that singin at the door?'

'I can't hear anything,' said the girl.

'Yes, there's someone there. Open the door and let him in.'

The girl had to open the door, and the frog hopped in and over to the fireside where the cat was sleeping. The frog sang, 'Gie me ma supper, ma promised wife, gie me ma supper, ma honey, ma dear.'

'What's this about you promisin tae marry him?' asked the mother.

'I don't know what he's on aboot,' said the girl. To quieten the frog she took a scone and crumbled it into milk on a plate and gave it to him. He ate it all. Then he sang, 'Gie me a kiss, ma promised wife, gie me a kiss, ma honey, ma dear.'

'Ah'm not kissin him!' said the girl, so loudly she woke up the cat. The cat woke up and saw a drop of milk at the corner of the frog's mouth and licked it off.

The frog turned into a fine strong tomcat.

He and the girl's cat had lots of kittens together.

Fitba Crazy

Track 6
Karaoke Track
34

This song is sung by adults as well as children. Some people say that it is an Irish song which was brought over to Scotland and changed.

1) You aa know my wee brither, his name is Jock McGraw,
He's lately jined a fitba club, for he's mad aboot fitba.
He has two black eyes already, and teeth lost frae his gub,
Since Jock became a member o that terrible fitba club.

CHORUS
For he's fitba crazy, he's fitba mad,
The fitba it has robbed him o the little bit o sense he had,
And it would take a dozen skivvies, his claes tae wash and scrub,
Since Jock became a member o that terrible fitba club.

2) The first game he took part in, I was there masel and saw,
There were jaickets for the goalposts and a tin can for the ba.
The Prince of Wales was there himsel, in his dinner suit,
Jock he passed the ball across, and shouted, 'CHARLIE,
SHOOT!'

3) His wife she says she'll leave him, if Jock he doesn't keep
Away from fitba kickin, at night time in his sleep.
He calls her Charlie Tully, and other names so droll,
Last night he kicked her out of bed and swore it was a goal.

4) In the middle of the field at Hampden, the captain said,
'McGraw,
Will you kindly take this penalty or we'll never win at aa.'
Jock took three steps backwards, and shot off from the mark.
The ball went sailin over the bar and landed in New York.

Songs keep going back and forward between Ireland and Scotland. Many people think that the famous song *Wild Mountain Thyme* is a Scottish song. This song was made famous by a group from Northern Ireland called the McPeake Family, and they say that the song was made up by Francis McPeake fifty years ago. However, the song is clearly based on the song *The Braes O' Balquidder* by the Scottish poet Robert Tannahill who lived in Paisley 200 years ago.

Ah the summertime is coming,
And the trees are sweetly blooming,
And the wild mountain thyme
Grows around the blooming heather.
Will you go, lassie, go?

And we'll all go together
To pull wild mountain thyme
All around the blooming heather.
Will you go, lassie, go?

From *Wild Mountain Thyme*

Now the summer is in prime,
Wi' the flowers richly bloomin',
An' the wild mountain thyme
A' the moorlands perfumin', –
Will ye go, lassie, go,
To the braes o' Balquidder?
Where the blaeberries grow
'Mang the bonnie bloomin' heather.

From *The Braes O' Balquidder*

Giant Fitba

There was a giant called Roddy MacSnoddy and he lived at the edge of Scotland, in a narrow place that is now called the Mull of Kintyre. One day he was bored and he called to his brother giant, Paddy MacRaddie, who lived over on the edge of Ireland.

'Hey, Paddy – how aboot a gemma fitba?'

'Fair play, ah'm up fur it,' said Paddy, 'but ah've nae ba – hiv you?'

'Naw, ah've none neither. That's right rotten. Hey, wait a meenit, we could jist use big lumpsa groond. Ah'll show ye – watch yer heid.'

Roddy lifted his size $96\frac{1}{2}$ tackety boot and kicked a great huge dod of earth and stone out of the edge of the land. It flew right across to Ireland. Paddy went to kick it back, but he missed and it went into the water.

'Here's another one, aim better this time,' said Roddy, and kicked another big lump out of the edge of Kintyre. But Paddy kicked that back into the water off Scotland too.

Paddy never got the hang of kicking straight, although he kept trying. Roddy got fed up after a while and went off to do something else, but Paddy kept practising.

If you want to know if this story is true, look at a map. The north of Ireland is full of lochs (spelt 'loughs') where Paddy kicked lumps out of the land, and off the west coast of Scotland are lots of islands that Paddy made with the land that he kicked. You'll see that there are hardly any islands off the north coast of Ireland, for Roddy had a better aim.

Roddy did miss one time, with a great lump of rock that landed just at the edge of Ireland's coast. You can go and see it. It's called the Giant's Causeway.

WORK SONGS

Many Scottish songs are about working life. Some were used while working – sailors sang rowing and rope-pulling songs, and girls sang songs when milking cows. In the Gaelic Song section (page 34) you will learn about waulking songs, used when shrinking tweed. Although work songs are about work, most Scottish work songs were not made especially to sing while working. Here, we give one song about whaling and another about coal mining. The bothy ballads on pages 18–21 are also work songs.

The Bonnie Ship The Diamond

Track 7
Karaoke Track
35

The Scots whaling ship, The Diamond, sailed from Peterhead in north-east Scotland nearly 200 years ago. She sailed to the Davis Strait between Greenland and Canada, heading for Baffin Bay where the whales could be caught.

1) The Diamond is a ship, ma lads, for the Davis Strait she's bound,
And the quay it is aa garnished wi bonnie lassies round.
Captain Thomson gives the order tae sail the oceans high,
Where the sun it never sets, ma lads, nor darkness dims the sky.

CHORUS
And it's cheer up, my lads, your hearts never fail,
When the bonnie ship The Diamond goes a-fishing for the whale.

2) Along the quays at Peterheid the lassies stand aroond,
Their shawls aa pulled aboot them and the salt tears rinnin doon.
Oh, don't you weep, my bonnie lass, though ye'll be left behind,
For the rose will grow on Greenland's ice before we change our mind.

3) Here's a health tae the Resolution, likewise the Eliza Swann,
Here's a health tae the Battler O Montrose, and The Diamond ship of fame.
We wear the troosers o the white, the jaickets o the blue,
When we return to Peterheid we'll be sweethairts wi you.

4) It'll be bricht baith day and nicht when the Greenland lads come hame,
Wi a ship that's full o oil, ma boys, and money tae oor name.
Here's a health unto The Diamond bright, the skipper and the crew,
Here's a health tae every bonnie lass that has a hairt so true.

The whalers would be away for several months, so their womenfolk dressed in their best shawls to see them off. The sailors boasted that when they came back they would be so rich that they would burn whale oil lamps during the day as well as at night.

In 1819, the ships named in this song were waiting for the pack ice to melt, but the wind changed and they were all caught and frozen in. The sailors knew this might happen and they had put tree trunks inside the hulls to make the ships stronger. One by one the ships were squeezed flat, but the sailors knew by the sounds that this was going to happen and they escaped onto the ice. They lived in tents made from the ships' sails and burnt their timbers for warmth. They suffered greatly but, after many months, they were rescued and brought home. They left The Diamond and the other ships behind, crushed flat by the Greenland ice.

The Hungry Cabin Boy

There was a boy who lived with his auntie who was cruel to him, so he stowed away on a whaling boat. He would creep out at night to take food from the ship's galley. The sailors caught him and wanted to punish him, but when they heard about his cruel auntie they felt sorry and let him stay to work as a cabin boy. Up in Baffin Bay they caught one whale and then another, but then they had no luck for weeks. The food stores were going done, and the cabin boy was always hungry.

One day a huge seagull landed on the deck. It had an injured wing, and the cabin boy rescued it, looked after it and mended its wing. When it was well, the seagull rose up in the air, went and caught a fish, and dropped it in front of the boy.

'Not another fish,' said the boy. 'I wish there was something else to eat.'

The seagull flew down, caught the boy's collar in its strong webbed feet and lifted him up, flying over the ocean. Far away they flew, to a hot land where curved yellow fruit and round orange fruit grew on strange trees, and sweet nuts grew under the ground. The boy ate till he was full, and fell asleep. Then the seagull took the cabin boy back to his ship. And flew away.

The Blantyre Explosion

On 22 October 1877 over two hundred miners were killed in a disaster at Dixon's Colliery, High Blantyre, near Hamilton in Lanarkshire. This song was made about the tragedy.

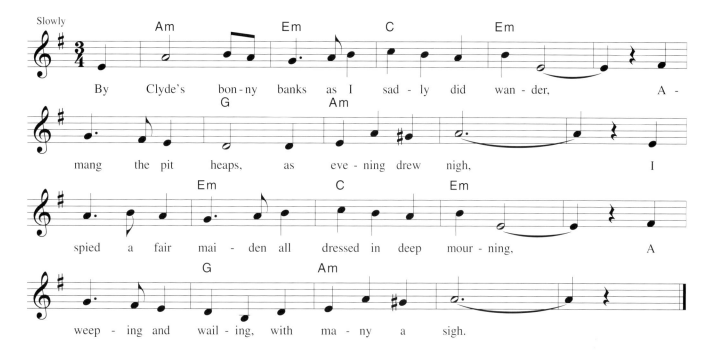

1) By Clyde's bonny banks as I sadly did wander,
Amang the pit heaps, as evening drew nigh,
I spied a fair maiden all dressed in deep mourning,
A weeping and wailing, with many a sigh.

2) I stepped up beside her, and thus I addressed her,
'Pray tell me, fair maid, of your trouble and pain.'
Sobbing and sighing, at last she did answer.
'Johnny Murphy, kind sir, was my true lover's name.

3) 'Twenty-one years of age, full of youth and good looking,
To work down the mines of High Blantyre he came.
The wedding was fixed, all the guests were invited,
That calm summer's evening young Johnny was slain.

4) 'The explosion was heard, all the women and children
With pale anxious faces made haste to the mine.
The news was made known, the hills rang with mourning.
Two hundred and ten young miners were slain.

5) 'Now children and wives, and sweethearts and parents,
That Blantyre explosion they'll never forget.
And all you young miners who hear my sad story,
Shed a tear for the victims who're laid to their rest.'

There are other Scottish songs about mining disasters, for example *The Donibristle Moss Moran Disaster*, which happened in Fife in 1901, and *The Auchengeich Disaster*, which happened as recently as 1957 near Stepps on the outskirts of Glasgow.

The Irish name of the girl's 'true lover' in *The Blantyre Explosion* is not surprising. Many Irishmen came over to Scotland in the 19th century to work in the pits and build canals. They often stayed to marry and raise families.

Mining life was so hard that to keep Scottish miners at their work they were legally treated as slaves, or serfs, right up until 1799. This meant they could not leave their employment without the permission of the coal owner, and their children were also obliged to work for him. Some even had to wear iron collars to show who they belonged to. In the wonderful Scottish love song *The Collier Laddie*, which was already an 'old' song in the time of Robert Burns, the girl chose a collier rather than a rich lord, so putting herself and her children into slavery.

Though you had all the sun shines on,
And the earth conceals sae lowly,
I'd turn my back on you and yours,
And embrace my collier laddie.

Love for love is the bargain for me,
Though the wee pit hoose should haud me
I'll mak my bed in the collier's neuk
And lie doon wi ma collier laddie.

From *The Collier Laddie*

David Down The Pit

In a village called Plean near Stirling in the 1920s lived a boy called David. His father was a miner, and so were the fathers of all his friends. One day, David's mother said, 'David, your father has left his piece behind. He'll be working all day with no food. Take this to the pithead and ask them can they send it down to him.'

David took the wrapped-up bread with butter, cheese and jam to the winding house with the big wheel above it, and said to the man who ran the cage, 'Hughie Reynolds has left this, can someone take it down to him?'

'Take it yourself,' said the cage man. David went into the metal cage, the cage man pulled a lever and David went falling for a long time down into the deep dark of the pit shaft. At the bottom, another man told David which way to go to through the tunnels to find his father.

It was warm and wet, and a long long way, sometimes dark and sometimes where men were working there was light. He met men he knew, who worked in pairs. Some were cutting the coal, some were shovelling coal into one wagon and stones into another. They would put a small metal token on top of each wagon to show which pair of men had filled it.

At last, when he asked again, a voice beside his knee said, 'Here I am, son.' His father was lying on his side in a pool of black oily water, wielding a pick that struck sparks off the stone, cutting away under the coalface.

David gave his father his piece, and went back though the dark tunnels.

He never went down into the black pit again. But he always told this story.

BOTHY BALLADS

A bothy is a building on a Scottish farm (especially in the area called Buchan in north-east Scotland) where the unmarried male workers lived in the days when the farms were worked by men with horses. A large farm might have had ten men living in the bothy. Four worked with the cattle and six with the horses.

In their leisure time, the men would sing songs, and some of these, which were about the work and life of the farms and the farmers, came to be called bothy ballads. The horsemen were considered superior to the 'coo workers' and most of the songs are about the horsemen's work.

The Barnyards of Delgaty

Track 9
Karaoke Track 36

1) As ah gaed doon tae Turra Merket,
Turra Merket fur tae fee,
Ah met in wi a wealthy fairmer,
The Barnyards o' Delgaty.

CHORUS
Linten adie, tooren adie,
Linten adie, Tooren ay,
Linten lowrin lowrin lowrin,
The Barnyards o' Delgaty.

2) He promised me the twa best horse
I ever set my een upon.
When ah gaed hame tae the Barnyards
There was nothin there but skin and bone.

3) The auld grey mare sat on her hunkers,
The auld dun horse lay in the grime.
For aa that I would 'hup' and cry,
They wouldna rise at yokin time.

4) When I gang tae the kirk on Sunday,
Mony's the bonny lass I see,
Sittin by her faither's side,
Winkin ower the pews at me.

5) Some can drink and no be drunk,
And some can fecht and no be slain.
I can coort anither man's lass,
And aye be welcome tae my ain.

6) Ma candle noo is fair brunt oot,
The snotter's fairly on the wane,
Fare ye weel, ye Barnyards,
Ye'll never catch me here again.

The young ploughman in *The Barnyards of Delgaty* went to Turra (Turriff) to 'fee', that is, to get employment on a farm for a fixed period of three or six months. The farmer promised two fine working horses, but he lied. The 'snotter' is the burnt wick of a candle.

Drumdelgie

Drumdelgie is another bothy ballad telling about the hard life of the farms.

There's a fairm toon up in Cai - rnie, It's kent baith far and wide, It's ca'd the Hash o Drum - del - gie, On bon - nie Dev - er - on - side, It's five o' - clock that we get up, And hur - ry doon the stair Tae get wir hor - ses fed wi corn, And like - wise straucht their hair.

1) There's a fairm toon up in Cairnie,
It's kent baith far and wide,
It's ca'd the Hash o Drumdelgie,
On bonnie Deveronside,
It's five o'clock that we get up,
And hurry doon the stair
Tae get wir horses fed wi corn,
And likewise straucht their hair.

2) Syne, after working half an hour,
Each tae the kitchen goes
Tae get started tae oor breakfast,
Which is generally brose.
At six o'clock the mill's put on,
Tae gie us a straucht work,
And twal o us has tae work at her
Till ye could wring oor sark.

3) The daylight it begins tae dawn,
The sky begins tae clear,
And the grieve he says,
'Hullo, my lads, ye'll stay nae langer here.
There's six o you'll gang tae the ploo,
And six tae caa the neeps,
And the owsen they'll be aifter you
Wi strae ropes roon their queets.'

4) The frost came on sae very thick
The ploo she wouldny go,
So we'd tae yoke the dung cairt
Amang the frost and snow.
But we will sing our horses' praise,
Though they be young and sma.
They far outshine the Broadland's anes
That gang sae full and braw.

The farm workers started work at 5am and had to feed and groom their horses before they got a breakfast of ground oats or split peas to which boiling water or milk had been added. Then twelve men had to turn the mill to grind more oats or peas. After that, they went outdoors to work, whatever the weather. Some went to plough the ground, others to cart turnips in from the field. The turnips were used for winter feed for the animals. But the plough could not be used in the frozen earth, so they had to cart dung to spread on the land instead.

Often the bothy ballads are critical of the farmer's strictness but mention the kindness of the 'kitchie deem', the young kitchen maid. The women farm workers lived in the farmhouse, not in the bothy. In turn, in songs such as *The Rovin Ploughboy* and *The Plooman Laddies*, the farmgirls admire the ploughmen.

Champion ploughboy, my Geordie lad,
Cups and medals and prizes o,
On bonnie Deveronside there is none can compare
Wi my jolly rovin ploughboy o.

From *The Rovin Ploughboy*

The Plooman Laddies

Doon yon-der den there's a ploo-man lad, Some sim-mer's day he'll be aa my ain. And sing lad-die aye, and sing lad-die o, The ploo-man lad-dies are aa the go.

1) Doon yonder den there's a plooman lad,
Some simmer's day he'll be aa my ain.

CHORUS
And sing laddie aye, and sing laddie o,
The plooman laddies are aa the go.

2) In yonder toon I could hae gotten a merchant,
But aa his gear wisna worth a groat.

3) In yonder toon I could hae gotten a miller,
But aa his dust wad hae mak me boak.

4) It's ilka time I gang tae the stack,
I hear his whip gie the ither crack.

5) I see him comin frae the toon,
Wi aa his ribbons hingin roon and roon.

Some of the songs, such as *Bogie's Bonnie Belle, When I Was New But Sweet Sixteen* and *Bonnie Ythanside*, tell of happy or unhappy courting on the farm.

When I was new but sweet sixteen, bonnie blythe and bloomin o,
It's little little did I think that at nineteen I'd be greetin o.

For the plooboy lads are gey braw lads, but fause and deceivin o.
They'll tak aa, and they'll gang awa, and leave their lassie grieving o.

For if I had kent what I noo ken, and ta'en ma mither's biddin o,
I wouldn't be sittin at your fireside, singin 'Heeshie baw, ma bairnie o.'

'It's heeshie baw, for ah'm yer maw, but the Lord kens wha's your daddie o,
But I'll tak good care, and I'll be aware o the young men and the gloamin o.'

When I Was New But Sweet Sixteen

Of course, many of the other songs and ballads in this book were also sung in the farm bothies, for example, *MacPherson's Rant, The Bonnie Ship The Diamond, The Gypsy Laddies* and *Johnnie O Breadislie*.

This is nae a sang o' love na', nor yet a sang o' money,
Faith it's naethin' verra peetifu', it's naethin' verra funny;
But there's Hielan' Scotch, Lowland Scotch, Butter Scotch and Honey,
If there's nane o' them for a' there's a mixture o' the three,
An' there's nae a word o' beef, brose, sowens, sauty bannocks na',
Nor pancakes, paes eggs for them wi' dainty stammicks;
But it's a' aboot a meal and ale that happened at Balmannocks,
McGinty's meal and ale, whaur the pig ga'ed on the spree.

They were howlin' in the kitchen like a caravan o' Tinkies, aye,
And some were playin' ping-pong and tiddely widdely winkies;
For up the howe and down the howe ye niver saw such jinkies,
As McGinty's meal and ale, whaur the pig ga'ed on the spree.

From *McGinty's Meal and Ale*

Many of the older bothy ballads were made up by farm workers themselves, but some later ones were made by singers such as G S Morris and Willie Kemp, who both became well-known recording artists and performers in music halls. G S Morris wrote the song *A Pair O' Nicky Tams* ('nicky tams' are a pair of leather straps that ploughmen wore around the bottoms of their trousers) and words for the old tune called *The Muckin' O' Geordie's Byre*. Willie Kemp wrote the tunes of favourite funny bothy ballads such as *McGinty's Meal And Ale*, about a pig who got drunk at a party, and *McFarlane O' The Sprots O' Burnieboosie*, about a man who sends his friend McFarlane to court a girl on his behalf.

The comic bothy ballads in particular are often full of words, pronunciations and phrases that are North-east speech. These can be hard to show in print. Look at the way G S Thomson spells the words in the first verse and chorus of his famous song *McGinty's Meal And Ale*.

The New Farmer and the Cream

A man had a dairy shop in the town. He thought he could make more money if he owned his own farm. So he bought a farm. The first day he walked round it, he saw that there were dishes of cream laid out in the cows' byre. He asked the farm workers what these were for.

'They are for the wee folk, to thank them for the help they give us in our work.'

'You may think you can cheat me because I am new here. You cannot. Put the cream back into the churn to be made into butter.'

The workers warned him the wee folk would be angry, but he would not listen. Next day, nothing went right on the farm. Equipment broke, the horses would not pull, butter would not come when the churn was turned and the cows would not come in at milking time.

That night, the workers begged the new farmer to let them put the cream out for the wee folk but he refused. The workers got most of the cows in, but there were two heifers left out up at the top of the highest field.

The farm workers said, 'We are sorry, sir. We are exhausted. They are your beasts, you must get them.'

The workers went into their bothy and lay down to sleep still wearing their work clothes.

The new farmer went up the hill, but the young cows would not be caught. All night he chased after them, over wall and through hedge, bruised and scratched. In the early morning mist he at last crept up close and reached out to get the tail of one, but it faded from his hand.

Down the hill he stumbled, and behind every tree and stone he heard small voices laughing. After that he let the workers put out the dishes of cream for the wee folk.

Narrative Songs

A narrative is a story. Bothy ballads, Scots ballads and some work songs tell a story and are therefore narrative songs too. However, *Rothesay-Oh*, *The Exciseman* and *MacPherson* represent traditional Scots songs which do not quite fit into the other song categories in this book, but which ought to be known about as well.

There are many songs that comment seriously on aspects of Scottish life or history. These include Jacobite songs, other historical songs such as *The Flowers of The Forest* and *A Parcel of Rogues*, social or work songs such as *Tramps and Hawkers* and *The Wark O The Weavers*, and many many drinking songs such as *Hame Drunk Cam I*, *Jock Stewart*, *Blue Blazing Blind Drunk* and *Willie Brew'd A Peck O Maut*.

The largest group of all is love songs. Traditional love songs or songs about love are not just about an emotion. They do not just say, 'I love you, love me too,' or, 'I love you but you don't love me,' or even, 'I used to love you but I don't any more.' They tell you the name of the person and where and what happened and why it happened. Examples include *The Bleacher Lass O Kelvinhaugh*, *The Road and the Miles to Dundee*, *The Bonnie Banks Of Loch Lomond* and *The Banks O Red Roses*.

Some dramatic narrative songs look pretty much like work songs or Scots ballads or bothy ballads but are not usually put under those headings. Perhaps they are not thought to be old enough to be ballads, or do not come from the north-east of Scotland where farm workers lived in bothies. Some examples are *The Gallawa Hills*, *The Lowlands of Holland* and *Hot Asphalt*.

MacPherson's Rant

Track 10

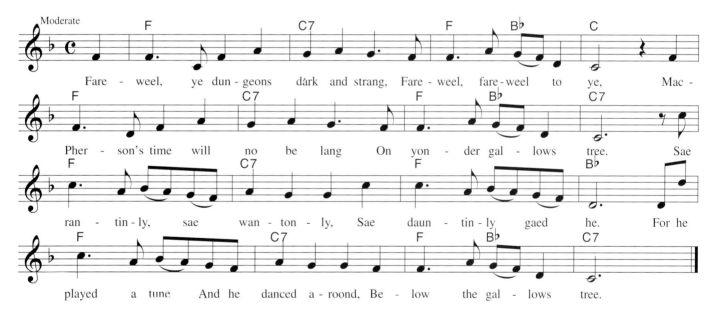

1) Fareweel, ye dungeons dark and strang,
Fareweel, fareweel to ye,
MacPherson's time will no be lang
On yonder gallows tree.

CHORUS
Sae rantinly, sae wantonly,
Sae dauntinly gaed he.
For he played a tune
And he danced aroond,
Below the gallows tree.

2) It was by a woman's treacherous hand
That I was condemned to dee.
For above a ledge at the window she sat
And a blanket she threw ower me.

3) There's some come here tae see me hang,
And some come tae buy my fiddle.
But before that I would part wi her
I'd brak her through the middle.

(omit chorus here)

4) And he took the fiddle intae baith o his hands
And he brak it ower a stane.
Sayin, 'Nae other hand shall play on thee
When I am dead and gane.'

5) The reprieve was comin ower the Brig o Banff
Tae set MacPherson free,
But they pit the clock a quarter afore,
And they hanged him frae the tree.

The story in the song is largely true. James MacPherson was an outlaw in the north-east of Scotland, one of the travelling people and the leader of a band of robbers. He was said to have been generous and popular with poor people, but he was an enemy of Lord Duff.

MacPherson was caught in Keith and hanged at the Cross of Banff on 16 November 1700. The story tells that no-one would arrest him because he was such a fine swordsman but as he came into Keith through a narrow street a woman sitting at a window overlooking the street threw down a thick heavy blanket which entangled him so he could not draw his sword. The court jury was packed with the dependants of Lord Duff, who found him guilty, but a friend of MacPherson rode to the higher court in Aberdeen for a pardon. The Laird saw the rider coming with the pardon and ordered the town clock to be put forward so that they could legally hang MacPherson before the pardon arrived.

MacPherson was a fine fiddler, and the night before he was hanged he composed this tune. He played it on the scaffold and then offered to give his fiddle to anyone who would play the tune at his wake. No-one would, so he smashed the fiddle. Anyone accepting it would have shown themselves to be a relative or friend of his, and so liable to arrest.

The Deil's Awa Wi' The Exciseman

Track 11
Karaoke Track
37

Scotland's most famous songwriter was Robert Burns. Here is one of his songs.

1) The Deil cam fiddlin thro' the town,
And danc'd awa wi' the Exciseman,
And ilka wife cries 'Auld Mahoun,
I wish you luck o' the prize, man!'

CHORUS
The Deil's awa, the Deil's awa,
The Deil's awa wi' the Exciseman!
He's danc'd awa, he's danc'd awa,
He's danc'd awa wi' the Exciseman!

2) 'We'll mak our maut, and we'll brew our drink,
We'll laugh, sing, and rejoice, man,
And monie braw thanks to the meikle black Deil,
That danc'd awa wi' the Exciseman.'

3) 'There's threesome reels, there's foursome reels,
There's hornpipes and strathspeys, man,
But the ae best dance ere cam to the land was
The Deil's Awa wi' the Exciseman!'

Robert Burns was born in 1759 in south-west Scotland. He wrote famous poems like *Tae A Mouse* and *Tam O Shanter*, and also songs like *Auld Lang Syne, Comin' Through the Rye* and *My Love is Like a Red, Red Rose*. Burns did not always write the words for his songs from scratch. Sometimes he took good songs being sung by the people around him and reworked them, or just wrote them down and got them published. Burns was as much a collector of traditional songs as he was a songwriter. Sadly, he had a short life, dying at the age of 37.

Like many other talented people, Robert Burns did not make his living from his art. One job he had was as an exciseman, collecting tax on whisky and other goods. The story goes that he and some other excisemen were sent to watch a suspicious-looking boat that had arrived in the Solway Firth. The excisemen saw that this was indeed a smugglers' vessel and that the crew were many, armed and likely to be dangerous. The excisemen knew that they would need more men to catch those on board the boat, so they sent to Dumfries for reinforcements. Burns was left with some men to try to prevent the boat landing or the crew escaping, even though he knew that they were too few to do this.

The messenger who was sent to Dumfries took a very long time to come back. One of the excisemen suggested that Burns write a song to pass the time. Burns went for a walk on the shingle. When he came back he recited this song. When the reinforcements eventually arrived from Dumfries, Burns was the first to board the smugglers' boat, sword in hand. The crew were captured and all the arms and stores of the vessel were sold at Dumfries.

Yet Burns' song says that he and his fellow excisemen were bad people who deserved to be taken away by the Devil, and that everyone would be so happy at this they would dance!

Robert The Bruce's March

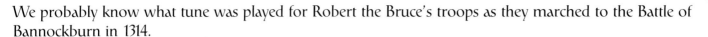

We probably know what tune was played for Robert the Bruce's troops as they marched to the Battle of Bannockburn in 1314.

Robert Burns wrote in a letter, 'There is a tradition, which I have met with in many places in Scotland, that (*Hey Tutti Taiti*) was Robert Bruce's March at the battle of Bannockburn.' Burns took this tune, slowed it down and wrote what 'one might suppose to be the gallant royal Scot's address to his heroic followers on that eventful morning.'

Hey Tutti Taiti is a very old tune. We do not have a document from 1314 that says the tune was used at Bannockburn. But there is, we are told, a document in a French château that says the tune was played as a march on 29 April 1429 when Joan of Arc entered the city of Orleans, and it was called a Scottish March then. It is still played as part of the annual Joan of Arc memorial celebrations in Orleans, where they call it *Marche des Soldats de R Bruce*, or *March of the Soldiers of Robert Bruce*.

Hey Tutti Taiti demonstrates the problems of trying to put a simple label on a tune. It was used as a march. It is in the form of a strathspey (a type of dance tune that you will find described later). Burns gave two sets of lyrics for the tune – he wrote *Scots Wha Hae*, and wrote or added to *Landlady, Count The Lawin*, a song about drinking all night. So *Hey Tutti Taiti* is a march, a strathspey dance tune, the tune of a patriotic song and a drinking song.

Scots, wha hae wi' Wallace bled,
Scots, wham Bruce has aften led,
Welcome to your gory bed,
Or to victorie!

Now's the day, and now's the hour:
See the front o' battle lour,
See approach proud Edward's power -
Chains and slaverie!

From *Scots Wha Hae* by Robert Burns

Landlady, Count The Lawin

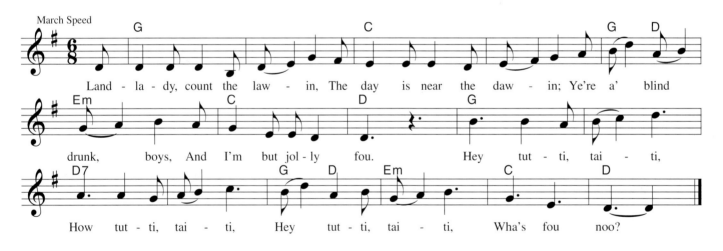

1) Landlady, count the lawin,
The day is near the dawin;
Ye're a' blind drunk, boys,
And I'm but jolly fou.

CHORUS
Hey tutti, taiti,
How tutti, taiti,
Hey tutti, taiti,
Wha's fou noo?

2) Cog, an ye were ay fou,
Cog, an ye were ay fou,
I wad sit and sing to you,
If ye were ay fou!

3) Weel may ye a' be!
Ill may ye never see!
God bless the king
And the companie!

The Day We Went Tae Rothesay-Oh

This song about a holiday trip on a steamer down the River Clyde to the island of Bute is full of jokes, and references to how people lived and had fun over 100 years ago.

Track 12

1) Wan Hogmanay at the Glasgow Fair, there was me masel and several mair,
We aa went off tae hae a tear and spend the day in Rothesay-oh.
We wandered doon the Broomielaw, through wind and rain and sleet and snaw,
And at forty meenits aifter twa we got the length o Rothesay-oh.

CHORUS
Durrum a doo a durrum a day, durrum a doo a daddy oh,
Durrum a doo a durrum a day, the day we went tae
Rothesay-oh.

2) A sodger lad caed Ruglen Will, wha's regiment lies at Barrenhill,
Went off wi a tanner tae buy a gill at a public hoose in Rothesay-oh.
He said, 'By God, I'd like tae sing.' I said, 'Ye'll no dae sic a thing.'
He said, 'Clear the floor and mak a ring and ah'll fecht yez aa in Rothesay-oh.'

3) In search o lodgins we did slide, tae find a place where we could bide,
There was eighty fowr o us inside a single end in Rothesay-oh.
We aa lay doon tae tak oor ease, when somebody happened for tae sneeze,
And he wakened a half a million fleas that et us alive in Rothesay-oh.

4) Some were bees, and some were bugs, and some had feet like dyers' clugs,
And they sat on the bed and they cockit their lugs, and they cried, 'Hurrah for Rothesay-oh.'
Ah said, 'Ah think we should elope.' So we went and jined the Band of Hope,
Ah, but the polis wouldny let us stop anither oor in Rothesay-oh.

Hogmanay is the 31st December, but the Glasgow Fair happens in the last two weeks of July. A 'tear' is a good time, a 'tanner' is sixpence in 'old' money and a gill is a very large glass of whisky. A 'single end' is a flat with only one room. 'Dyers clugs' are wooden clogs worn by workers who dyed cloth. To join the Band of Hope, a temperance organisation, you had to swear you would never drink alcohol any more.

The pleasure steamers carried people to Rothesay from the Broomielaw in the middle of Glasgow. They went down the River Clyde to Rothesay and other places, and this was called going 'doon the watter'.

Like *Fitba Crazy*, this song would have been sung in 'music halls'. These started off as rooms in public houses where people could go and hear old and new songs. Later, music halls were built in the cities and towns of Scotland. In these, audiences could enjoy not just singers and musicians but also other types of performances like recitations and dancing.

Some music hall singers wrote their own songs. A few became famous. The best known was Harry Lauder, whose records sold all over the world. Many of his songs are still popular today – *Roamin In the Gloamin*, *I Love a Lassie* and *A Wee Deoch An Dorus*. Another very popular performer was Will Fyffe, who wrote *Sailing Up The Clyde* and many others. His best known song was *I Belong to Glasgow*. However, he actually belonged to Dundee!

Scotland is rich in comic songs, but the trouble with humour is that most jokes go out of date and need to be re-explained to new generations, just like some of the jokes in Shakespeare's plays. The most popular comic Scottish songs today are usually quite new, by present-day songwriters. For example, Adam McNaughtan wrote *The Jeely Piece Song*, Matt McGinn wrote *The Red Yo-Yo* and John Watt wrote *The Keltie Clippie*. However, some comic bothy ballads and music hall songs are still popular.

The Worser

Our Rothesay song tells of a happening at the Glasgow Fair, when all the people of Glasgow would be on holiday for the last two weeks of July. There are still the amusement 'shows' each year on Glasgow Green, but there used to be theatres in tents and exhibitions of strange things as well. One year, hung over a tent was the sign 'A Shilling to see the Worser'. The people had never heard of a worser, so they paid their shillings and went in.

The showman drew back a curtain and showed them a pig.

The people said, 'That's a pig. We know what a pig looks like. You're a cheat.'

The showman said, 'Good people, wait a while and listen. Look at this pig. Is it not a beautiful pig?' The people agreed it was a very fine pig; fat and sleek and healthy.

He then showed a second pig, which was a good strong pig but rather thinner and not as fine as the first one. Then he showed a third pig that was scrawny and sickly.

'Now,' he said. 'This first pig is a very fine pig. This second one is worse than the first. But the third pig is by far a worser!'

The people had to agree. They told all their friends to go and see the Worser, so they would get caught too.

BALLADS

There are two ways the word 'ballad' is used when talking about Scottish songs. One is as a general word for a song or poem that tells a story using short verses. But 'ballad' is also a specialised word for one of a group of songs that are hundreds of years old, and tell dramatic stories of war, love, betrayal, magic, trickery and strange events.

No-one knows who made up these ballads. Some have had their words and tunes changed by many different singers over the centuries, so that it can be hard to recognise that two songs are versions of the same ballad. Perhaps only a few lines are shared, but the story is the same.

Here is a ballad that is said to be about Lady Jean Hamilton, the wife of the Earl of Cassilis, who lived in Culzean Castle, Ayrshire, in the 1620s. But there are many versions of this song known in other English-speaking countries. For example, in England there is a version called *The Raggle Taggle Gypsies*, while in the USA the ballad is sometimes called *Blackjack Davie*. In this version, the gypsies cast a spell over the lady of the castle and she goes with them, but they are caught and hanged. Below we give eight verses of the ballad from the singing of Jeannie Robertson.

The CD version of *Gypsy Laddies* is sung by the great Aberdeenshire traditional singer Jeannie Robertson, one of the Travelling People. Her fine versions of ballads and songs became widely admired and sung in Britain and the USA. She was awarded the MBE in 1968 and died in 1975.

The Gypsy Laddies

Track 13

1) Three gypsies came tae oor ha door,
An oh but they sang bonny oh.
They sang so sweet and too complete,
That they stole the heart of our lady oh.

2) For she cam tripping down the stairs,
Her maidens too before her oh,
And when they saw her weel faured face
They throwed their spell oot owre her oh.

3) When her good lord came home that night
He was askin for his lady oh,
But the answer the servants gave tae him,
'She's awa wi the gypsy laddies oh'.

4) 'Gae saddle tae me my bonnie, bonnie black,
My broon it's ne'er sae speedy oh,
That I may go ridin this long summer day
In search of my true lady oh.'

5) For the very last night that I crossed this river
I had dukes and lords to attend me oh.
But this night I must put in ma warm feet an wade,
An the gypsies widin before me oh.

6) Last night I lay in a good feather bed,
My own wedded lord beside me oh.
Tonight I must lie in a cauld corn barn,
An the gypsies lyin aroun me oh.

7) For it's will you give up your houses and your lands,
An will you give up your baby oh?
An will you give up your own wedded lord
An keep followin the gypsy laddies oh?

8) For there are seven brothers of us all,
We are wondrous bonnie oh,
But this very night we all shall be hanged
For the stealin of the earl's lady oh.

There are many other very well-known traditional ballads. Some are about historical events and people in Scotland, for example, *The Baron of Brackley*, *Johnnie Armstrong*, *The Battle of Harlaw* and *The Bonny Earl of Murray*. Sometimes traditional ballads are thought of as poetry rather than songs, and are taught in school in English lessons, because mostly they were first printed without any tune being given.

Ballads quickly get right to the heart of a story. In the very first verse of *The Baron of Brackley*, the baron's enemy is at his gates challenging him to a fight to the death.

Ballads can have long or short versions – a shocking part of the story found in one version may be left out altogether in another.

Doon Deeside cam Inverey whistlin and playin,
And he was at Brackley's yetts ere the day was dawin.
'And are ye there, Brackley, and are ye within?
There's shairp swords are at your yetts, will gar your blood spin.'

From *The Baron Of Brackley*

The Queen's Four Maries as widely sung has only a few verses, set in Edinburgh, in which Mary Hamilton laments that she is to die, without explaining why. Longer versions have eighteen or twenty-five verses, telling that she had a child by the King of Scotland and had killed it. The 'auld queen' has heard the baby crying, and takes Mary Hamilton to Edinburgh to be executed. As she walks down the Canongate, part of the Royal Mile between Edinburgh Castle and Holyrood Palace, Mary says, 'Little did my mither think the day she cradled me, the lands I was to travel in, the death I was to dee.'

The ballad is precise about names, but it was Mary Queen of Scots who had four Maries as maids of honour and they were named Mary Fleming, Mary Seaton, Mary Beaton and Mary Livingston. None of them suffered such a death.

The Queen's Four Maries

Slowly

Yest-reen the Queen had four Mar-ies, the nicht she'll hae but three. There was Ma-ry Sea-ton, and Ma-ry Bea-ton and Ma-ry Car-mich-ael and me.

Johnnie O Breadislie

This is another very Scottish ballad. It tells how Johnnie went out to hunt the royal deer and was chased and wounded by the King's Foresters. One version of the ballad says it happened in Durrisdeer in Dumfriesshire, another places it in Monymusk in Aberdeenshire. In some versions Johnnie is killed, in others he escapes.

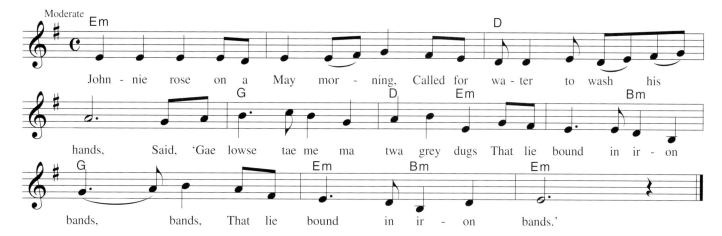

1) Johnnie rose on a May morning,
Called for water to wash his hands,
Said, 'Gae lowse tae me ma twa grey dugs
That lie bound in iron bands, bands,
That lie bound in iron bands.'

2) When Johnnie's mother, she heard o this,
Her hands wi dule she wrang,
Says, 'Johnnie, for yer venison
Tae the greenwoods dinna gang, gang,
Tae the greenwoods dinna gang.'

3) But Johnnie has breasted his guid bent bow
And his arras one by one,
And he's awa tae the gay greenwood
Tae ding the dun deer doon.

4) Johnnie shot, the dun deer lap,
She was wounded in her side,
And atween the water and the wood
The greyhounds laid her pride.

5) Johnnie ate o the venison,
And the dugs drank o the bleed,
And they lay doon and fell asleep,
Asleep as tho they were deid.

6) Then by there cam a silly auld man
And a silly auld man wis he,
For he's awa tae Monymusk
The foresters for tae see.

7) Up then spak the Chief Forester,
And an angry man wis he,
'If this be Johnnie O Breadislie,
My faith, we'll gar him dee.'

8) 'Stand fast, stand fast, my noble steed,
Stand fast and dinna flee.
Lie close, lie close, my guid greyhounds
And we will gar them dee.'

9) Johnnie shot the six of them
And the seventh he's wounded sair,
And he swung his heuch ower his horse's back,
And he swore that he'd hunt mair.

Other ballads are Scottish versions of ballads which are also known in England, the USA and sometimes in Scandinavia.

There is often an element of magic in the traditional ballads, for example, in *The Two Sisters*, *The Demon Lover*, *Tam Lin* and *Thomas The Rhymer*. One of *The Two Sisters* drowns the other because they both love the same young man. The drowned sister's body floats away – the miller who finds it uses her bones to make a fiddle or a harp, her hair becomes the strings. When the instrument is played at the wedding of the other sister and the young man, it tells of the murder. *The Demon Lover* comes back from the dead and takes his sweetheart away. Both *Tam Lin* and *Thomas The Rhymer* are stolen away by the Queen of the Fairies.

The Great Silkie of Sule Skerry

The Great Silkie of Sule Skerry is a sealman who lives on one of the remote rocky islands called skerries. A human girl has a baby by him.

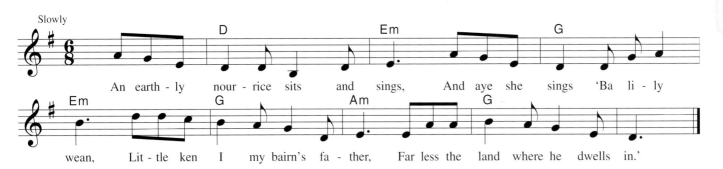

An earth-ly nour-rice sits and sings, And aye she sings 'Ba li-ly wean, Lit-tle ken I my bairn's fa-ther, Far less the land where he dwells in.'

1) An earthly nourrice sits and sings,
And aye she sings 'Ba lily wean,
Little ken I my bairn's father,
Far less the land where he dwells in.'

2) Then up he came to her bed foot,
Aye, a grumblie guest was he,
Saying 'Here am I, thy bairn's father,
Although I be not comely.

3) 'I am a man upon the land,
I am a silkie on the sea,
And when I'm far frae every strand,
My home it is in Sule Skerry.'

4) He has ta'en a purse of gold,
And he has placed it upon her knee,
Saying, 'Give to me my little young son,
And take thee up thy nurse's fee.

5) 'And it shall come on a summer's day,
When the sun shines bright on every stane,
I'll come and fetch my little young son,
And teach him how to swim the faem.

6) 'And you shall marry a gunner good,
A right fine gunner I'm sure he'll be,
And the very first shot that e'er he shoots
Will kill both my young son and me.'

JACOBITE SONGS

The Jacobites were the supporters of King James the VII of Scotland and II of England, of his son James 'The Old Pretender' and of his grandson Prince Charles Edward Stuart 'The Young Pretender' (also known as Bonny Prince Charlie). There are many Gaelic Jacobite songs which were composed at the time, but most Jacobite songs in Scots were written long after the Uprisings of 1715 and 1745.

Skye Boat Song, or Speed Bonnie Boat

Track 15

This is the best-known Jacobite song, but it is in fact quite recent. The words were written by an Englishman, Sir Harold Boulton, about 120 years ago. He used an 'iorram', a Gaelic rowing song format, and the tune is said to come from the Gaelic song *Cuachan nan Craobh*, or *The Cuckoo in the Grove*.

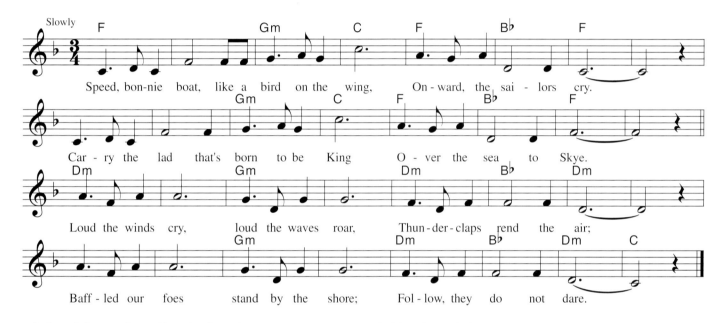

1) Speed, bonnie boat, like a bird on the wing,
Onward, the sailors cry.
Carry the lad that's born to be King
Over the sea to Skye.

2) Loud the winds cry, loud the waves roar,
Thunderclaps rend the air;
Baffled our foes stand by the shore;
Follow, they do not dare.

3) Many's the lad fought on that day
Well the claymore could wield,
When the night came silently lay
Dead on Culloden's field.

4) Burned are our homes, exile and death
Scatter the loyal men,
Yet ere the sword cool in the sheath
Scotland will rise again.

Robert Burns, Lady Caroline Nairne and James Hogg all wrote Jacobite songs. They rewrote old songs or made new ones based on old models. Burns published *It Was A' For Our Rightfu' King*, *The Highland Widow's Lament* and a song about love called *Charlie He's My Darling*. Lady Nairne wrote lyrics for *Wi A Hundred Pipers* and *Will Ye No Come Back Again?* She also wrote a more warlike set of words entitled *Charlie Is My Darling*. Hogg wrote Jacobite lyrics for *The Sherramuir March* (see page 46), *Wha Wouldna Fecht For Charlie* (see page 51) and many others.

Hey Johnnie Cope

When he was in Dunbar, the English general Sir John Cope sent a challenge to Prince Charlie who was in Edinburgh. The two armies fought at Prestonpans (where there were small coalpits as well as salt pans). Cope was beaten and had to flee. This song was written by Adam Skirving, who lived near Prestonpans at the time.

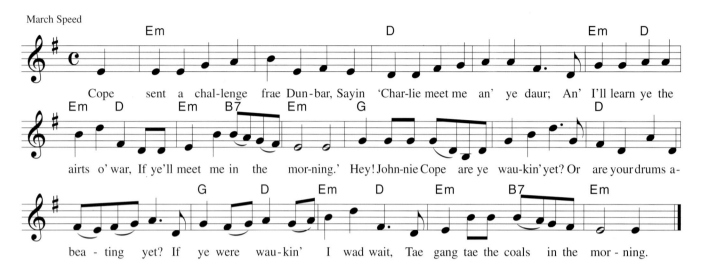

1) Cope sent a challenge frae Dunbar,
Sayin 'Charlie meet me an' ye daur;
An' I'll learn ye the airts o' war,
If ye'll meet me in the morning.'

CHORUS
Hey! Johnnie Cope are ye waukin' yet?
Or are your drums a-beating yet?
If ye were waukin' I wad wait,
Tae gang tae the coals in the morning.

2) When Charlie looked the letter upon,
He drew his sword its scabbard from,
'Come, follow me, my merry men,
And we'll meet Johnnie Cope in the morning.'

3) Now Johnnie, be as good as your word,
Come, let us try baith fire and sword,
And dinna flee like a frichted bird,
That's chased frae its nest i' the morning.

4) When Johnnie Cope he heard o' this,
He thocht it wouldna be amiss,
Tae hae a horse in readiness,
Tae flee awa in the morning.

5) Fye now, Johnnie, get up an' rin,
The Highland bagpipes mak' a din,
It's better tae sleep in a hale skin,
For it will be a bluidie morning.

6) When Johnnie Cope tae Dunbar cam,
They speired at him, 'Where's a' your men?'
'The de'il confound me gin I ken,
For I left them a' in the morning.'

7) Now Johnnie, troth ye werena blate,
Tae come wi' news o' your ain defeat,
And leave your men in sic a strait,
Sae early in the morning.

8) 'In faith', quo Johnnie, 'I got sic flegs
Wi' their claymores an' philabegs,
Gin I face them again, de'il brak my legs,
So I wish you a' good morning.'

GAELIC SONG

Gaelic Song

Gaelic is the old language of most of Scotland, but now those who speak it are mainly from the Hebrides and the north-west mainland. There are many fine songs in the Gaelic language. In this section, we look at waulking songs, psalm singing and mouth music. The sections on marches (pages 46–47) and pipe music (pages 49–51) tell a little about tunes made by Gaels.

The oldest Gaelic songs are about the legendary heroes of the Fianna and go back over a thousand years. For hundreds of years the clan chiefs supported their own poets and musicians. In the last three hundred years many other fine composers have created Gaelic songs and tunes, and new songs are still being made and sung today.

There is a very strong tradition of choral and solo singing in Gaelic song. Harmonisation, however, was not part of the tradition but was introduced among the competitions at an annual festival called the Mod.

English language versions of Gaelic songs made by Marjory Kennedy-Fraser or Hugh Roberton became very popular early in the 20th century. But the meanings, or even the styles, of the songs were often changed. For example, *Kishmul's Galley* as translated and arranged by Marjory Kennedy-Fraser is a slow and very dramatic ballad, but in the original it is a vigorous 'waulking song'.

Waulking Songs

Waulking songs were used by groups of women who had gathered to help shrink newly woven tweed by beating the wet cloth on a table. In these short excerpts from two waulking songs from the island of Barra, recorded in the 1960s, the women were pounding a dry blanket instead of a length of wet tweed. You can hear on the recording how the song helps the hard work be enjoyable.

The refrain 'Eile le ho ró ho hù o' has no meaning!

Robh Thu sa Bheinn?

Were You In The Mountains?

Track 16(a)

Le d'ghun - na snaip o ho hu o Eile le ho ró ho hù o

Le d'ghunna snaip o ho hu o
Your snap-lock gun ...

CHORUS
Eile le ho ró ho hù o (Ail-uh leh-ho ro ho hoo-oh)

Ortho ghualainn o ho hu o
... on your shoulder

Dol a shealg na
H-èilde ruaidheadh.
On your way to hunt the red hind.

Eala cha dig
Slàn o d'luaidhe.
The swan cannot survive your shot.

Mo Rùn Ailein

My Love Alan

Dh'èir - ich mi moch ó hò Mo rùn Ail - ein ó hò

Mo rùn Ailein ó hò
My love Alan

CHORUS 1
Mo rùn Ailein ó hò (Mu roon ellain oh haw)

Dh'èirich mi moch, ó hò
Maduinn earraich
Dhìrich mi suas
Gual a' bhealaich
Shuidh mi air cnoc
Leig mi m'anail
I rose early on a spring morning. I climbed the shoulder of the hill-pass. I sat on a knoll and rested.

Dh'amhairc mi bhuam
Fad mo sheallaidh
Chunnacas do long
Mhòr 'san t-seanail
Cò bh'air a stiùir
Ach mo leannan!
I looked into the distance as far as I could see; I saw your great ship in the channel; who was at the helm but my lover!

CHORUS 2
Chall o éile ó hò

Chan iomair mi, ó hò
Ard chan èigh mi
Cha tèid mise
'N còir na clèitheadh.
I will not ply the cloth, I will not raise a shout, I will not go near the waulking-board.

The Seal Wife

A young fisherman was among the rocks collecting shellfish for bait. He heard a strange swishing sound, and saw a young woman running on the sand. Her long black hair hung down to cover her nakedness, except for a seal skin that was on her calves and feet. The skin made the odd noise in the sand and slowed her. She took it off and hid it beneath a rock, and ran on.

The fisherman crept out, stole the skin and went away for an hour. When he returned the girl was sitting by the rock, weeping salt tears. He said, 'Oh, lass, I see you are come ashore from a shipwreck. Here, have my coat to keep you from the weather.'

He took her back to his little black house, for he had fallen in love with her. Soon she fell in love with him, and the two were married and they had a daughter.

On a day, the daughter was left alone in the house and she looked into her father's chest that no-one but he might touch. At the bottom of the chest she touched something that felt alive. It was a skin, warm and soft. She put it around her, and it seemed that she was swimming under the sea.

Her mother came in, and said, 'My skin!' and took it from the girl and ran away down to the ocean. When the fisherman came home, he found his daughter crying, and when he understood what had happened he ran down to the water and called to his wife. But she never came home.

Gaelic Psalms

Hymns and psalms can be sung in Gaelic or English in Scottish churches. There is a very powerful old style of unaccompanied psalm singing which is still heard in some Gaelic-speaking churches. The first two lines, having been read out by the leader (usually the minister), are sung by the precentor (the person that leads the singing) and the congregation joins in gradually. Then the precentor chants the next line and the congregation repeats it, with varying degrees of ornamentation and at varying speeds. Each subsequent line is similarly treated to the end of the verses selected. Although each singer is singing the same tune, the effect is a continuous sound with different chordal effects created within it.

This style (called polyphony) of singing psalms goes back to the Reformation in the 16th century. It was once widespread throughout England and other countries but is now found only in churches where the minister preaches in Gaelic.

Psalm 46 (verses 1 and 2)

Tune: Stroudwater

Track 17

This psalm was recorded in a church in Lewis, with Donald MacLeod leading the singing. Here are the basic notes of the tune but, as you can hear from the CD, it would be very hard to fit the words on this page exactly to the notes.

'Se Dia a's tearmunn duinn gu beachd,
Ar spionnadh e 's ar treis:
An aimsir carraid agus teinn,
Ar cabhair e ro-dheas.

Mar sin ged ghluaist' an talamh trom.
Cha'n aobhar eagail duinn;
Ged thilgeadh fòs na slèibhte mòr'
Am builsgein fairg' is tuinn.

God is our refuge and strength, a very present help in trouble.
Therefore will we not fear, though the earth be removed,
And though the mountains be carried into the midst of the sea.

Gaelic Vocal Dance Music

known as Mouth Music (Puirt A Beul)

When people want to dance but musical instruments are not available, they need a song in which the lively rhythm is more important than the story behind the words. Such dance songs are used around the world, but puirt a beul have particular qualities of neatness and energy, and the tongue-tripping lyrics are performed so quickly and deftly that it can be hard to tell where the singer is pausing to breathe.

Dòmhnall Dubh

Track 18(a)

Dòmhnall Dubh an Dòmhnallaich a-nochd an tòir air
Mòr a'Cheannaich
Dòmhnall Dubh an Dòmhnallaich a-nochd an tòir air
Mòrag.
(2 times)

Ibhi abhi Ibhi ābhi, air do shlàinte Mhòr a'Cheannaich
Ibhi abhi Ibhi ābhi, air do shlàinte, Mhòrag,
Ibhi abhi Ibhi ābhi, air do shlàinte, Mhòr a'Cheannaich
Dòmhnall Dubh an Dòmhnallaich a-nochd an tòir air Mòrag.

'S ioma rud tha dhìth orm a dh'fheumainn fhìn man
dèanainn banais
'S ioma rud tha dhìth orm a dh'fheumainn fhìn mam pòsainn.
(2 times)

Ibhi abhi Ibhi ābhi …
'S ioma rud tha dhìth orm a dh'fheumainn fhìn mam pòsainn.

Dh'òlainn fhìn is dhannsainn fhìn air oidhche banais
Mòr a'Cheannaich
Dh'òlainn fhìn is dhannsainn fhìn air oidhche banais
Mòrag.
(2 times)

Ibhi abhi Ibhi ābhi …
Dh'òlainn fhìn is dhannsainn fhìn air oidhche banais Mòrag.

**Black Donald MacDonald is tonight pursuing Mòr,
the merchant's daughter. 'Your good health, Morag.'**

**'I need many things before I can arrange a wedding,
before I can marry. I would drink and I would dance
on the night of Mòr's wedding.'**

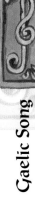

Nighean Na Cailliche

Track 18(b)

Nighean na cailliche crotaiche crūbaich, thionndadh i
cūlaibh 's throideadh i rium;
Bhreabadh i casan mu seach air an ūrlar, 's thionndadh i
cūlaibh 's throideadh i rium.
(2 times)

Thionndadh i cūlaibh, thionndadh i cūlaibh, thionndadh i
cūlaibh, throideadh i rium *(3 times)*
Nighean na caillich' as miosa san dūthaich, thionndadh i
cūlaibh 's throideadh i rium.
(2 times)

**Daughter of the hump-backed bent old hag, she would turn her back (on me) and scold me; she would
stamp her feet, turn about on the floor and turn her back and scold.**

The Loch of the Sword

The old boundaries of three Highland counties met in the middle of a small loch called The Lochan of the
Sword, or Loch-na-Clive. It got that name 400 years ago.

For years, the chiefs of two clans argued about where the limits of their lands lay. At last Cameron of Lochiel
and Murray of Atholl agreed they would meet alone to negotiate. As Lochiel went to the meeting place, an
old woman called out to him, 'Lochiel, where are your dogs?'

'I am not going hunting, I have no need of dogs today,' he answered.

'You will need dogs today, go find some.'

Lochiel collected thirty men. He told them to hide in the heather and not to show themselves unless he
opened his cloak to show its bright red lining. Then he went on.

At first, the two chiefs agreed, but then they quarrelled. At last, Murray of Atholl drew his basket-hilted
sword and waved it in the air, and from the heather above his side of the lochan rose twenty armed men
who came running down the brae. 'Who are these men?' asked Lochiel.

'Not men, just Atholl sheep come to eat the fine grass of this place,' said Murray.

Cameron of Lochiel opened his cloak to show the scarlet lining, and thirty men ran down to meet him.
'Who are these men?' asked Murray.

'Not men, just Lochiel dogs to make sure your
Atholl sheep eat only where they have a right to,'
said Cameron.

Murray laughed, and held his sword
high. Then he threw it deep into the
lochan and said, 'Let us make peace,
and agree our boundary is here.'
They did so.

Traditional Scottish Music

Scottish Dance Music

Reels, Strathspeys and Jigs

In Scotland, dance and song live close together. The Irish grannie got taken to a ball. The wee gallus bloke came by the dancin to meet the girls. The devil danced away with the exciseman. James MacPherson danced as he played his new tune. Gaelic and Scots mouth music songs were used for dancing to.

The best-known types of Scottish country dances are the reel, the strathspey and the jig. There are many kinds of reels – threesomes, foursomes and eightsomes – and many different sets of dance steps and 'figures' which are danced to strathspeys and jigs. These are given such names as *Cadgers In The Canongate* and *Off She Goes In The North*. The jig *Strip The Willow* is danced by up to twenty people in two long lines facing each other.

March tunes are used for some Scottish country dances, like *The Gay Gordons* which is danced by couples. *The Dashing White Sergeant* is danced by two groups of three, and there are dances with surprising titles such as *The Circassian Circle*. (Circassia is a place north of the eastern Black Sea next to Russia.)

REELS

The reel is the fastest of all the tunes played on traditional instruments in Scotland. It is generally in 4/4 or 2/4 time, meaning that it has 4 or 2 beats in each bar. Reels are usually made up mainly of quavers, as in this example. Reels can be played on many instruments but are most commonly associated with the fiddle, upon

which fast tunes can be played very easily. Although it is a very old form of music, the reel has retained its popularity and many people are composing reels today. Some of these have been given unusual titles, such as *The Whisky Meniscus* composed by Colin Campbell.

Below is a well-known reel.

Soldier's Joy

Track 30(d)

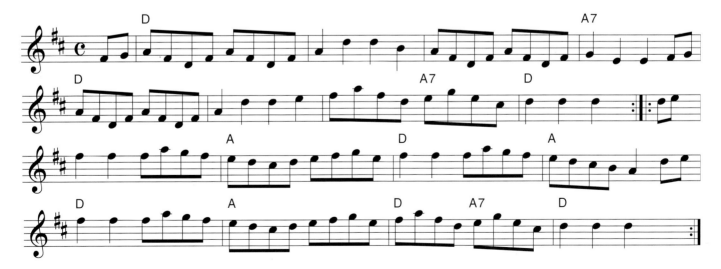

Mrs MacLeod of Raasay

One of the best-known Scottish reel tunes has different names in different countries. In Scotland we call it *Mrs MacLeod of Raasay*. We do not know anything about Mrs MacLeod, but it was the fashion for composers to name new tunes or rename old tunes after important people they wanted to compliment. This reel seems to be based on the old march and song *The Campbells Are Coming*.

Mrs MacLeod is used for mouth music songs (see page 37) in both Gaelic and Scots. One of the songs is a translation from the Gaelic original.

> MacPhee turn the cattle round Loch Avornin. *(3 times)*
> Here and there and everywhere the kye are in the corn.
>
> Waitin at the sheilin, Mairi Bhan mochree,
> Waitin at the sheilin, far awa tae sea.
> Home will come the bonny boats, Mairi Bhan mochree,
> Home will come the bonny boys, Mairi Bhan mochree.

Another song uses only the first part of the tune.

> The black bull's broken oot an eaten aa the corn. *(3 times)*
> Ah winna bide tae Saturday, ah'll away the morn.

Other favourite reels include *The Mason's Apron, The Fairy Dance, The East Neuk of Fife, The Reel of Tulloch, The Wind that Shakes the Barley* and *The High Road to Linton*.

STRATHSPEYS

The strathspey takes its name from the Strathspey area (the strath or broad glen of the river Spey) of north-east Scotland. It was written originally for the fiddle and used for dancing. Nowadays, the strathspey is played on many different instruments. It is in 4/4 or common time and it sounds quite different to the reel because it contains many dotted rhythms.

One of these rhythms has a special name, the 'Scotch snap'. A Scotch snap consists of a very short note immediately followed by a longer note, giving a 'snap' sound when played. The Scotch snap often looks like this in written music.

Earl Grey

Track 20

This classic strathspey was composed by James Hill who lived in Gateshead, near Newcastle, England, but was born in Dundee. Hill is best remembered for his hornpipes such as *The Bee's Wing* and *The High Level*. Charles, Earl Grey (1764-1845), from Falloden in Northumberland, was a British prime minister who was considered a hero because of his great Reform Bill of 1832, which gave the vote to many more people.

Country Dancing

You may meet two differing approaches to dancing reels, strathspeys and jigs. At events run by Scottish Country Dance societies, there may be quite strict rules about how the dances should go, what the dancers should wear and whether you can call out or yell while you dance. A Scottish country dance band is likely to include one or two accordionists, a fiddler, a double bass or bass guitar player, a drummer who plays in a 'military' style, and a piano or keyboard player.

At ceilidh dances you will usually find a much more relaxed approach to the music, dances and clothing. A ceilidh dance band is likely to use rock drum rhythms and to have an electric guitar and bass, pipes and an electronic keyboard, as well as an accordion and a fiddle.

Tracks 21 & 31

CD tracks 21 and 31 show the difference between the two band styles. On track 21, Craig McCallum's band play in the Country Dance Band style, with two accordions, a fiddle, keyboards, drums and a bass. Track 31 is a ceilidh band style combination of fiddle, whistle, concertina, accordion, highland pipes, guitar, bass guitar and drums, led by fiddler and songwriter Brian McNeill. This band is playing a set of reels called *The Atlantic Reels* which Brian McNeill himself composed.

John McAlpine

Strathspeys

This tune is very versatile. It is popular as a strathspey but, when the Scotch snap is 'ironed out', it is also used as a march, a polka and a song tune.

A ballad, *The False Knight On The Road*, in which a schoolboy meets the devil who tries to trick him with hard questions, is sung to this tune. Another song sung to this tune is *The Bog Down In The Valley*, which begins with 'a tree in the bog' and adds things such as the branch on the tree and the limb on the branch, eventually ending with the nest with an egg, the bird inside it, the feather of the bird and the spot on the feather! All the elements are added together to make a very long 'cumulative' song.

The strathspey is danced as a 'longways set', with lines of men and women facing each other and interweaving across the central floor space in different patterns.

The ancient tune *Hey Tutti Taitie* is a strathspey, although Robert Burns slowed it down when he used it for *Scots Wha Hae*.

JIGS

The jig is usually in 6/8 time and is used for Scottish dances such as *Strip the Willow*. This type of tune can be played on a variety of instruments such as fiddles, bagpipes and accordions. Jigs are also found in many other countries, especially Ireland.

They are played quite quickly with sequences of quavers in groups of three – see the illustration. When you listen to a jig, you may hear it

as six fast beats in the bar or as two slow pulses. Listen out for this in *Merrily Danced the Quaker's Wife*, a very old tune (it has been suggested that it can be traced back 600 years).

Merrily Danced The Quaker's Wife

Track 22

The Cock O The North

Track 23

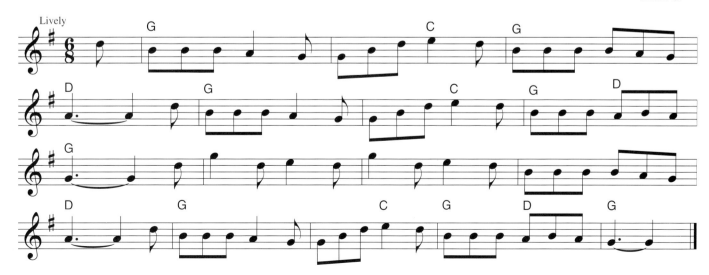

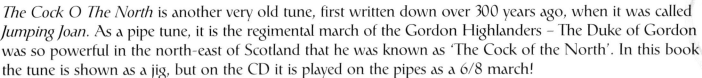

The Cock O The North is another very old tune, first written down over 300 years ago, when it was called *Jumping Joan*. As a pipe tune, it is the regimental march of the Gordon Highlanders – The Duke of Gordon was so powerful in the north-east of Scotland that he was known as 'The Cock of the North'. In this book the tune is shown as a jig, but on the CD it is played on the pipes as a 6/8 march!

In 1897, the Gordon Highlanders were fighting in Afghanistan. They were attacking uphill at a place called the Heights of Dargai. The soldiers were led by their pipers, one of whom, George Findlater, was shot through both legs. He propped himself up against a rock and carried on playing this tune to encourage the soldiers to go on. Piper Findlater was awarded the Victoria Cross, but he did not at first get an army pension. He performed in music halls, telling his story and playing his pipes until the government changed its mind.

The Cock O The North has also had words fitted to it, but they are rather too rude to print here.

Pentatonic Tunes

Pentatonic tunes are very common in Scotland and other countries.

Western scales usually have 7 notes. The pentatonic scale, however, has only 5 – the 4th and 7th notes are never present. This means that no semitones occur in the

pentatonic scale (some people think that this makes the pentatonic scale sound pure). For example: the Western scale of C major runs C, D, E, F, G, A, B; whereas the pentatonic scale, when beginning on C, runs C, D, E, G, A.

An easy way to work out the pentatonic scale is to play on the black keys of a piano beginning on F sharp and ending on D sharp. *Speed Bonnie Boat* and *Auld Lang Syne* are both examples of pentatonic tunes.

Waltzes

Speed Bonnie Boat on page 32 is a good example of a waltz. Waltzes are played in many other countries but are also popular in Scotland. The waltz, a fairly slow dance with 3 beats in the bar, is normally danced by couples. If you've ever been to a ceilidh, you will know that the last dance of the evening is usually a waltz. Other examples of waltzes include *I Belong to Glasgow* and *The Northern Lights of Old Aberdeen*. Like *Speed Bonnie Boat*, these waltzes are songs and it is quite common for people to sing the words whilst they are dancing.

Marches

Marches were, of course, composed for fighters to march along to, so they have a regular stress in 2/4 or 4/4 time. Some Scottish pipe marches are very old indeed. When regiments were formed in the Highlands, they had pipers and drummers to march to, and the pipers made up many marches and other pipe tunes. These musicians were formed into pipe bands (see page 51).

Marches are now often used for dancing. On CD track 21, Craig McCallum's band play three marches for the dance called *The Gay Gordons*.

Sherramuir March, or The Stewarts March

This jaunty march has a long and complex history.

Let MacIntyres say what they may,
Let MacIntyres say what they may,
We'll take and keep the good old way,
Let them say their will oh.

From *Gabhaidh Sinn An Rathad Mór*

The tune we give has two parts, but the original pipe march has nine parts. In Gaelic it is called *Gabhaidh Sinn An Rathad Mór*, which means *We Will Take The High Road*. The pipe march first belonged to the MacIntyres of Cruachan in Argyll, but was taken and claimed as their own by the Stewarts of Appin some 500 years ago. The Stewarts played it when they went home from the Battle of Pinkie in 1547. The Gaelic name and lyric relates to the Battle of Inverlochy in 1644.

The march was played again by the Stewarts of Perthshire on 13 November 1715 at the Battle of Sheriffmuir, near Dunblane, where the march got its English name.

That battle was part of the 1715 Uprising, fought between the Highland clans, led by the Earl of Mar, and the Hanoverian government forces, led by the Duke of Argyll. No-one could agree who won the battle. Later on, a lyric about the Battle of Sheriffmuir was put to the pipe tune by James Hogg.

Will ye gang tae Sheriffmuir, Bold John o Innisture?
There to see the noble Mar and his Highland laddies.
Aa the true men o the north, Angus, Huntly and Seaforth,
Scouring on to cross the Forth wi their white cockadies.

By James Hogg

Later still, the tune began to be used for Scottish children's songs, the best known of which is called *Katie Bairdie*. At last, about 120 years ago, it went down to England where they took out the Scotch snap and changed an old children's song to fit the Scottish tune. Try singing or playing the first part of the tune with all the bouncing dotted quaver and semiquaver notes turned to an even rhythm of quavers. You will find the tune becomes *London Bridge Is Falling Down*!

The Barren Rocks of Aden

This march tune is associated with the Gordon Highlanders regiment, and is played for the dance called *The Gay Gordons*. (Our Scottish Country Dance Band set of marches is for dancing *The Gay Gordons*.) The tune is said to have been composed by a piper who was delighted that his regiment was leaving the hot dry port of Aden in what is now South Yemen in Arabia.

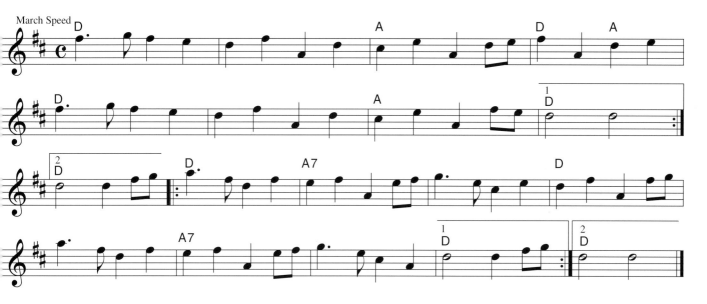

The Bloody Fields of Flanders

The Bloody Fields of Flanders is a pipe march version of an old Perthshire song tune. Two famous Scottish songs, *Scotland The Brave* and *The Freedom-Come-All-Ye*, are set to versions of the march tune. We have written it in 4/4 time below, but the piper on the CD is playing it as a 3/4 march.

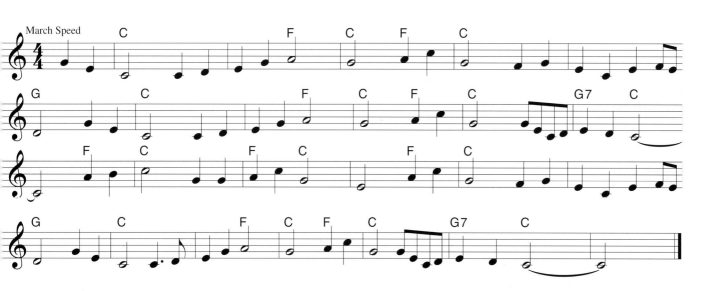

The Siege of Carlisle

In 1745 the Jacobite army was heading south from Scotland to Carlisle. The garrison of Carlisle Castle consisted of eighty army pensioners. When they heard the Scots were coming, they fired bravely at anything they saw — cows, sheep and horses. But when the Scots arrived and began to play their secret weapon, the bagpipes, the garrison of Carlisle became so afraid they surrendered!

SLOW AIRS

MacPherson's Rant (see page 22) is an example of a slow air. Slow airs are often played on the fiddle but, unlike reels and strathspeys, they are not used for dancing. There are no special rhythms associated with slow airs – they are simply tunes played slowly. It is very common in Scots fiddle music to find a slow air followed by a march, a strathspey and then a reel. This is called a 'set' of tunes, and it allows the fiddler to play tunes that gradually get faster, often leading to a fast and furious finish.

The Cradle Song was written by J Scott Skinner after seeing a sick child being cared for by his mother in a hotel in Forres. *Farewell To Whisky* was written by Niel Gow in 1799 because in that year the barley harvest was so poor that the use of it for making whisky was banned. You can read more about Skinner and Gow on page 52.

Other famous slow airs include *Niel Gow's Lament for the Death of his Second Wife, Roslin Castle, The Rowan Tree, The Bonnie Lass O Bon Accord, The Flower O The Quern* and *The Flooers O The Forest*.

The Cradle Song

Track 30(a)

Farewell To Whisky

Track 25

PIPE MUSIC

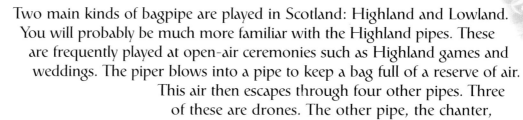

Two main kinds of bagpipe are played in Scotland: Highland and Lowland. You will probably be much more familiar with the Highland pipes. These are frequently played at open-air ceremonies such as Highland games and weddings. The piper blows into a pipe to keep a bag full of a reserve of air. This air then escapes through four other pipes. Three of these are drones. The other pipe, the chanter, is fingered by the piper to play the melody. Two tenor drones play Bb one octave below the chanter, and the bass drone produces Bb an octave lower still.

The Lowland pipes differ in that, instead of blowing into a pipe to fill the bag, the piper uses his arm to press bellows. Also, the Lowland piper usually sits down, whereas the Highland piper stands and often will march up and down as he plays. The Lowland pipes are often called the 'cauld wind' pipes since they receive cold air, rather than warm air from the mouth. The Lowland pipes have a quieter sound than the Highland pipes and are more suited to playing indoors.

Both types of pipes can be used to play such music as waltzes, reels, jigs, marches and slow airs. These kinds of music are known as 'Ceòl Beag', meaning 'little music'.

The classical music of the Highland pipes is called Ceòl Mór (great music) or Pibroch (piping). Ceòl Mór includes salutes (tunes addressed to someone of importance), gatherings (tunes used to gather members of a clan), laments (tunes expressing sadness at someone's death) and tunes connected with historical events.

Pibroch is played only on the Highland pipes, by a solo piper. In order to play it, you have to be a very good piper. Piping teachers will generally let their pupils start learning pibroch only when they have become very accomplished, and some pipers will never learn to play pibroch.

Pibroch sounds quite slow and sombre and it can take a long time to play one piece from beginning to end.

The Highland Bagpipe

Pibroch

A pibroch begins with a theme (called an ùrlar, or ground) which is then varied throughout the piece. These variations become gradually more complex and rhythmic as the piece goes on. At the very end, the basic theme is played again.

One thing that makes the variations of a pibroch more complex is the amount of ornamentation that the piper must play. Ornamentation consists of 'grace notes' that are not part of the main melody. These notes are essential to all pipe music. In the examples below, the small notes are the grace notes and the large notes are the main melody. You will also see that the time signature changes between and within variations. Because of the amount of ornamentation, we can only show a few bars of some of the variations. We give the first few bars of the ùrlar, which has 16 bars, and parts of three of the seven variations which are played in this tune.

On our CD recording, you will hear the first 6 bars only of the ùrlar, followed by the same 6-bar 'line' played in the seven variations, then the ùrlar again to finish. The order of performance is: ùrlar, dithis, dithis doubling, taorluath, taorluath doubling, crunluath, crunluath doubling, crunluath mach, then ùrlar again.

The tune *I Got A Kiss Of The King's Hand* is said to have been composed in 1651 by a member of the famous piping family, the MacCrimmons of Skye. When King Charles II held a review of the Scottish army at Stirling, he was told that MacCrimmon was known as the Prince of Pipers, and the king let the piper kiss his hand. The piper was so pleased he composed this tune on the spot.

I Got A Kiss Of The King's Hand

Track 26

Ùrlar

Dithis

Taorluath

Crunluath

Pipe Bands

The Highland pipes are also to be heard playing in Scottish pipe bands. These bands were first formed by Scottish regiments, but then bands were formed in police forces, by commercial companies, towns and other groups. Today such bands of pipers and drummers can be found in countries all over the world.

There is no fixed number of pipers or drummers in a pipe band. There are three kinds of drums – snare, tenor and bass. The drumming can be very complex and syncopated, and is much admired by drummers from other countries, who call it 'Scottish Jazz'. Band members are usually dressed in full Highland dress, which consists of kilts, jackets and caps.

Pipe bands march to the music they play, so it is not surprising they often play marches. On CD track 27, the Pipes and Drums of the 1st Battalion The Black Watch play two Jacobite song tunes: *Ye Jacobites By Name* and *Wha Wouldna Fecht For Charlie*, or *The 42nd*. The song tune for *Wha Wouldna Fecht For Charlie* is given below – the version on the CD has been adapted for pipes.

Wha Wouldna Fecht For Charlie, or The 42nd

Track 27

This march has an old Jacobite lyric, which was either collected or made by James Hogg (we do not know which).

Wha saw the 42nd,
Wha saw them gaun awa,
Wha saw the 42nd
Merchin doon the Broomielaw?

Some o them had boots and stockins,
Some o them had nane at aa,
Some o them had a wee drap whisky
For tae keep the cold awa.

Wha wouldna fecht for Charlie,
Wha wouldna draw the sword,
Wha wouldna up and rally
At the Royal Prince's word?

Think on Scotia's ancient heroes,
Think on foreign foes repelled,
Think on glorious Bruce and Wallace,
Wha the proud usurpers quelled.

By James Hogg

More recently, other words (also to do with soldiers going off to war) have been used.

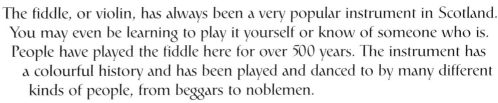

THE FIDDLE

The Fiddle

The fiddle, or violin, has always been a very popular instrument in Scotland. You may even be learning to play it yourself or know of someone who is. People have played the fiddle here for over 500 years. The instrument has a colourful history and has been played and danced to by many different kinds of people, from beggars to noblemen.

The instrument has four strings, tuned G, D, A, E starting from the lowest note up, and is played with a bow. The fiddle itself is made of wood and, in the olden days, the strings were made of animal gut and the bow was made of horsehair. The fiddle can play both fast and slow tunes equally well.

There have been many famous fiddlers over the years in Scotland. Niel Gow (1727-1807) lived in Perthshire, and played at dances along with his brother Donald who played the cello. Niel Gow composed many famous pieces including *Athole Brose* and *Farewell to Whisky*.

From the village of Fochabers in Morayshire came William Marshall (1748-1833) whom Burns described as the 'first composer of strathspeys of the age'. Marshall wrote music that was more difficult to play, and this pushed fiddlers to learn new technical skills. Like many other composers, Marshall often named tunes after particular people or places. Two such tunes are *The Marquis of Huntly's Farewell* and *Balvenie Castle*.

Later came James Scott Skinner (1843-1927), from Banchory, also in north-east Scotland. He played in many concerts and became a well-known personality. He also made recordings that were issued as gramophone records and were popular all over Scotland. Skinner wrote simple tunes such as *The Cradle Song* – a beautiful slow air – but also very complicated, showy pieces such as *The President*.

The Hen's March To The Midden

Track 28

This is a very old showpiece tune for the fiddle. You can hear the fiddle imitating the sound of the hen cackling as it marches.

52 | Leckie & Leckie

THE ACCORDION

The accordion is another popular instrument in Scotland, often played along with the fiddle at accordion and fiddle clubs. A famous accordion and fiddle duo are Phil Cunningham (accordion) and Aly Bain (fiddle). The accordion is a much more modern instrument than the clarsach, bagpipes or fiddle, having arrived in Scotland from Europe in the 19th century. The accordion is quite a loud instrument and can easily be heard at dances without being amplified. It can play

most of the types of Scottish music described in this book – slow airs, marches, jigs, strathspeys and reels – and is the favourite instrument for dance music in north-east Scotland.

There are two kinds of accordion: one is called the 'piano accordion' because it has keys like those of a piano; the other is called the 'button key accordion' because it has much smaller keys which are in the shape of small buttons. Most Scottish accordionists play the piano accordion, and this is the type of accordion that you normally find playing in a Scottish Country Dance Band.

There are also smaller relatives of the accordion which have fewer buttons: the melodeon and the concertina.

THE CLARSACH

The clarsach, also known as the small harp, is one of Scotland's oldest instruments. The main difference between the clarsach and the concert harps you may have seen playing in orchestras is in size: the clarsach is smaller and can be quite easily carried from place to place. The clarsach also has no pedals, so it can be difficult to change quickly from one key to another.

In the olden days, long fingernails were required to play the clarsach. Many of those who played it were blind (perhaps because they were not able to take part in hard jobs, such as farming, which would result in broken fingernails).

The clarsach has a quiet sound (unlike the Highland pipes!) and in the past was often used for lulling people to sleep. Very little original music for the clarsach survives in Scotland, so clarsach players nowadays tend to play tunes such as reels, strathspeys and marches which are common to other instruments. The clarsach also goes very well with the voice and is often used to accompany singing. *The Lea Rig*, played on the CD, is an old song which was reworked by Robert Burns.

Track 29

OTHER INSTRUMENTS

The piano and now the electronic keyboard are often used in bands or to accompany a solo fiddler or singer. You will hear electronic keyboard played on several of our CD tracks.

The piano or keyboard is commonly used to accompany fiddle music and to give a strong beat to country dance music. The keyboard player in a Scottish country dance band will play in a style called 'vamping', which usually means playing one note with the left hand and a three-note chord with the right hand, giving an 'oom-pah' rhythm.

Another instrument, often used by people starting to learn to play Scottish tunes, is the mouth organ (or harmonica), known in Scotland as the 'mouthie'. The 'penny whistle' and the flute are also popular.

The gut and wire strung guitar was used in Scottish music 200 years ago, then fell out of fashion. The wire-strung acoustic guitar has been brought back in the last fifty years to accompany songs and tunes. Performers such as Archie Fisher, Dick Gaughan and Tony McManus have created a distinctively Scottish style of intricate and melodic guitar playing. The Shetland guitarist Peerie Willy Johnson created a jazzy chordal way of accompanying fiddle tunes which is now much imitated.

More modern bands use electronic versions of the fiddle, the guitar and the bass.

There are many other instruments in use in Scottish traditional music. The bodhrán is a large Irish circular drum which is held with one hand and hit with a beater. Banjos, with either four or five strings, and eight-stringed mandolins are sometimes heard.

The unusual-sounding instrument played on *The Day We Went Tae Rothesay-Oh* is called a trump, jaws harp or Jew's harp. This is a very old instrument and is played all over the world. It is made of metal or wood and is very easy to play.

You may be surprised to hear the cello being played on some song tracks, since the cello is thought of as a 'classical instrument' only, but this too has a history of use in Scottish music. Two hundred years ago, a favoured combination for Scottish dance music was two fiddles and a cello.

AULD LANG SYNE

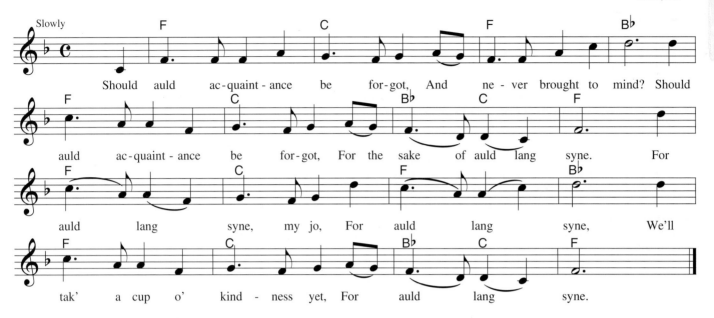

1) Should auld acquaintance be forgot,
And never brought to mind?
Should auld acquaintance be forgot,
For the sake of auld lang syne.

CHORUS
For auld lang syne, my jo,
For auld lang syne.
We'll tak' a cup o' kindness yet,
For auld lang syne.

2) And surely ye'll be your pint stowp!
And surely I'll be mine!
And we'll tak' a cup o' kindness yet,
For auld lang syne.

3) We twa hae run about the braes
And pu'd the gowans fine,
But we've wandered many a weary fit,
Sin auld lang syne.

4) We twa hae paddl'd in the burn
Frae morning sun till dine,
But seas between us braid hae roar'd
Sin auld lang syne.

5) And here's a hand my trusty freend
And gie's a hand o' thine!
And we'll tak' a richt gude-willy waught
For auld lang syne!

This is another pentatonic tune. Robert Burns wrote that he had heard the first verse of this song from an old man, and immediately wrote it down as he thought it 'exceedingly expressive'. He later remarked that it 'has often thrilled through my soul.'

Burns added the other verses given above and wanted to print the song in the collection of songs called the *Scots Musical Museum*, but he had already used the tune the old man sang for another song called *O Can Ye Labor Lea*, also known as *I Fee'd a Man at Martinmas*. Instead, Burns' lyrics were attached to another old tune. Burns called this tune *The Miller's Wedding*. This tune has had many other names and has even been claimed as an English tune, but the Scottish claim seems incontestable.

We still sing *Auld Lang Syne* to the tune *The Miller's Wedding*. So the best-known Scottish song is not sung to the original tune, but to another traditional tune. Verses 1, 3 and 5 of *Auld Lang Syne* are sung on CD track 32.

MODERN TIMES

Auld Lang Syne has been carried around the world, and is sung at New Year in many lands. Sometimes Burns' words are used, sometimes the text has been translated into the local language.

Scottish country dancing can be found throughout the world, and many Scots performers of traditional music and song make their living performing in North America or continental Europe and seldom perform at home.

Fiddle playing has recently become even more popular. Groups called Strathspey and Reel Societies, and Fiddle and Box Clubs have met and organised events for many years. Now you can also find informal 'sessions' of fiddlers and accompanying musicians playing for their own pleasure in pubs. This way of playing is copied from Ireland and often concentrates on Irish, rather than Scottish, tunes. Famous fiddlers nowadays include Aly Bain, who is from Shetland where many people play the instrument and many fine tunes have been made.

Some well-respected traditional singers are Jock Duncan, Archie Fisher, Ray Fisher, Dick Gaughan, Christine Kydd, Gordeanna McCulloch, Alistair McDonald, Iain MacKintosh, Dougie MacLean, Flora MacNeil, Brian McNeill, Christine Primrose, Jean Redpath, Sheila Stewart and Sheena Wellington.

Here are some well-known Scottish musicians – Aly Bain, Phil Cunningham, Duncan Chisholm, Ivan Drever, Alasdair Fraser, Carmen Higgins, Gordon Mooney, Tony McManus and Rab Wallace.

Many Scots singers have also become well known as songwriters writing in the style of traditional songs – Gill Bowman, Sheila Douglas, Robin Laing, Matt McGinn, Adam McNaughtan, Nancy Nicolson, Andy M Stewart and John Watt.

Groups who have made a name for themselves at home and abroad include The Battlefield Band, Capercaillie, Ceolbeg, Chantan, The MacCalmans, Old Blind Dogs, Ossian, Rock Salt And Nails, Sileas, The Tannahill Weavers, Tannas, The Whistlebinkies, Wolfstone and The Wrigley Sisters.

Many Scots who began performing traditional Scottish or other music in folk clubs or festivals have gone on to success in other areas: Eric Bogle, Billy Connolly, Barbara Dickson, John Martyn, Robert Noakes and Isla St Clair.

Musical influences from other parts of the world and elements of rock and popular music have been incorporated in the music of Afro-Celtic Sound System, Martyn Bennett, Salsa Celtica and Shooglenifty.

These days, we expect to hear songs accompanied by musical instruments, but this is fairly new in Scotland. Songs were mostly sung unaccompanied, and some traditional singers still do this. In recent years, the instrumental accompaniments and arrangements have become more skilled and complex, and audiences are not expected to sing the chorus as they used to. Dance tunes are sometimes played at a speed that would trip any dancer up. But some performers still insist on the tune tempos being right for dancing, and encourage the audience to join in singing the choruses.

Glossary & Listings

GLOSSARY OF GREAT SCOTTISH WORDS

Some of these words also have other meanings. We give here the meaning as used in the songs in this book.

A

aa – all
ae – one
afore – before
ah'll – I will
aifter – after
ain – own
aince – once
airts – directions
aleerie – holding the knee bent
amang – among
anes – once
anither – another
aroond – around
arras – arrows
atween – between
auld – old
awa – away

B

ba – ball
ba lily – hush
backsword – *see* claymore
bairn – child
baith – both
baloo – hush
bannock – a flat round cake of oatmeal
bawbee – a halfpenny
bide – stay
blate – shy
bleed – blood
bluidie – bloody
boak – be sick
brae – a steep road *or* hillside
braid – broad
brak – broke
braw – fine, good-looking
breid – bread
brig – bridge
brither – brother
broon – brown
brose – oatmeal with boiling water or milk
brunt – burnt
bunnet – soft flat brimless peaked cap
byre – cowshed

C

ca – cart home from the fields
ca'ed – called
cairt – cart
cam – came
cauld – cold
ceilidh – in north Scotland, an informal social evening; in south Scotland, an organised evening of dancing
clarsach – small harp
claymore – the Great Sword (so long it was carried on the back and swung with both hands)
cockadie – a cockade (a rosette, or bunch of ribbons worn on a hat)
cockit – cocked
cog – drinking bowl
corbies – carrion crows

D

dae – do
daur – dare
dawin – dawning
dee – die
deid – dead
deil *or* de'il – devil
dine – dinner time
ding – strike *or* defeat
dinna – do not
dirks – daggers
doo – dove, pigeon
doon – down
drap – drop
dugs – dogs
dule – grief
dun – greyish-brown
dyers' clugs – dyers' clogs

E

een – eyes
e'er *or* ere – before *or* ever
et – ate

F

faem – foam
fairm toon – substantial group of farm buildings
faured – favoured
fecht – fight
fee – to agree to work for a fixed period
Fianna – mythological heroes of Scotland from Gaelic legend
fit – foot
fitba – football
flegs – frights
fowr – four
frae – from
frichted – frightened
fu – full *or* drunk

G

gae – go
gaed – went
gallant – fine-looking man
gallus – bold, cheeky
gang – go
gar – make
gaun – going
gie – give
gie's – give me
gill – old measure of liquid
gloamin – twilight
gowans – daisies
greetin – weeping
grieve – head workman of a farm
groat – (formerly) silver coin worth fourpence, (now) nothing at all
groond – ground
grumblie – grim
gub – mouth
gude-willy – good will
guid – good
gutty – rubber (*from* 'gutta percha')

H

ha – hall
hae – have
hairt – heart
hale – whole
hame – home
hauds – holds
heeshie baw – hush-a-bye
heid – head
heilan – highland
heuch – thigh
hingin – hanging
Hogmanay – New Year's Eve
Hogmanany – New Year's Day
hoonds – hounds
hoose – house
howe – low piece of land, glen
hunkers – haunches

I

ilka – each
intae – into
ither – other

J

jaicket – jacket
jined – joined
jinkies – high jinks
jo – good friend

K

ken or kenned or kent – knew
kirk – church
kye – cows

L

lang – long
lang syne – long ago
lap – leapt
lawin – bill to be paid
loast – lost
lowse – loosen or untie
lugs – ears

M

Mahoun – name for the Devil
mair – more
mak – make
mammy – mother
masel – myself
maut – malt whisky
maw – mother
mazzie – mother
meal and ale – party with oatmeal
    and beer
meenit – minute
meikle – see muckle
merchin – marching
merket – market
mither – mother
mochree – darling, beloved
monie – many
muckle – much, large

N

na – no
naethin – nothing
nane – none
natter – chat
neeps – turnips
ne'er – never
neuk – corner
nicky tams – leather straps round the
    bottom of trousers

no – not
nourrice – nurse

O

o or o' – of
oor – hour or our
oot – out
ower or owre – over
owsen – oxen

P

paes eggs – hard-boiled eggs, used at
    Easter
peetifu – pitiful
philabeg – kilt
piece – portion of food
pit – put
ploo – plough
polis – police
pu'd – pulled

Q

queets – fetlocks

R

rant – a lively tune or song
rantinly – merrily
reel – dance tune
richt – right or very
rickle – collection or pile
roon – round

S

sae – so
sair – sore or severely
sang – song
sark – shirt
saunt – saint
sauty – salty
scouring – driving
screiching – screaming
shairp – sharp
sheilin – summer dwelling
sic – such
silkie – seal
sin – since
single end – one-room flat
skint – skinned or penniless
skivvies – people who do menial
    work
sma – small
snaw – snow
snotter – end of a candle wick
sodger – soldier

sowens – oat husks and fine meal
    steeped in water
spak – spoke
speired – asked
stack – pile of wood, peats, etc
stane – stone
stowp – tankard
strae – straw
strait – predicament
strang – strong
strathspey – a type of dance
Strath Spey – a place in north-east
    Scotland
straucht – straight, straighten
strides – trousers
stummicks – stomachs
syne – ago

T

tae – to
taen – taken
tak – take
tanner – sixpence
targes – round shields
tear – jaunt
troth – pledged word
Turra – Turriff
twa or twae – two
twal – twelve

V

verra – very

W

wan – one
waught – swig
waukin – wakening
weel – well
werena – were not
wha – who
whaur – where
wi – with
wide – wade
widin – wading
winna – will not
wir – our
wis – was
wouldna – would not

Y

ye – you
ye's – you (plural)
yer – your or you're
yetts – gates

LISTING OF CD TRACKS

1) *Coulter's Candy* – Katherine Campbell & Ewan McVicar
2) *Today is Hogmanay* – Katherine Campbell & Ewan McVicar
3) *One Two Three Aleerie* – Katherine Campbell
4) *Wee Gallus Bloke* – Ewan McVicar
5) *The World Must Be Coming To An End* – Katherine Campbell & Ewan McVicar
6) *Fitba Crazy* – Ewan McVicar
7) *The Bonnie Ship The Diamond* – Ewan McVicar & Katherine Campbell
8) *The Blantyre Explosion* – Katherine Campbell
9) *The Barnyards of Delgaty* – Ewan McVicar
10) *MacPherson's Rant* – Ewan McVicar & Colin Campbell
11) *The Deil's Awa Wi' The Exciseman* – Katherine & Colin Campbell
12) *The Day We Went Tae Rothesay-Oh* – Ewan McVicar
13) *The Gypsy Laddies* – Jeannie Robertson, from *The Muckle Sangs*, Scottish Tradition 5, CDTRAX 9005
14) *Johnnie O Breadislie* – Katherine Campbell
15) *Skye Boat Song* (or *Speed Bonnie Boat*) – Katherine Campbell
16) *Robh Thu sa Bheinn* and *Mo Rūn Ailein* – Miss Mary Morrison and Chorus, from *Waulking Songs From Barra*, Scottish Tradition 3, CDTRAX 9003
17) *Psalm 46*, Stroudwater – Donald MacLeod and Congregation, from *Gaelic Psalms From Lewis*, Scottish Tradition 6, CDTRAX 9006
18) Puirt A Beul: *Dōmhnall Dubh* and *Nighean Na Cailliche* – from *Seonag NicCoinnich (Joan MacKenzie)*, Scottish Tradition 19, CDTRAX 9019
19) *Mrs MacLeod of Raasay* – Colin & Katherine Campbell
20) *Earl Grey* – Colin & Katherine Campbell
21) Scottish Country Dance Band Set: *Campbell's Farewell To Red Castle*, *Corriechoillies* and *Bonnie Ann* – The Craig McCallum Scottish Dance Band, from *In A Different Light*, CDTRAX 037
22) *Merrily Danced The Quaker's Wife* – Mary Kennedy
23) *The Cock O The North* – Josh Dickson
24) *The Bloody Fields of Flanders* – Josh Dickson
25) *Farewell To Whisky* – Colin & Katherine Campbell
26) *I Got A Kiss Of The King's Hand* – Josh Dickson
27) Pipe Band Set: *Ye Jacobites By Name* and *Wha Wouldna Fecht For Charlie* – The Pipes and Drums of the 1st Battalion The Black Watch, from *The Ladies From Hell*, CDTRAX 162
28) *The Hen's March To The Midden* – Colin & Katherine Campbell
29) *The Lea Rig* – Julia Lane of Castlebay, from *Tapestry II In A Garden Green*, CMT2D
30) Air, March, Strathspey and Reel Set: *Cradle Song, Barren Rocks of Aden, John McAlpine* and *Soldier's Joy* – Colin & Katherine Campbell
31) Ceilidh Band Set: *The Yesterman's Hand* and *The Old Man's Answer* – Brian McNeill and friends, from *Back o the North Wind*, CDTRAX 047
32) *Auld Lang Syne* – Katherine Campbell

KARAOKE TRACKS
33) *Wee Gallus Bloke*
34) *Fitba Crazy*
35) *The Bonnie Ship The Diamond*
36) *The Barnyards of Delgaty*
37) *The Deil's Awa Wi' The Exciseman*

Vocals, keyboard, cello – Katherine Campbell
Vocals, guitar, mouth organ, Jew's harp – Ewan McVicar
Pipes – Josh Dickson   Fiddle – Colin Campbell
Accordion – Mary Kennedy   Clarsach – Julia Lane

SONGS AND TUNES

Many of the songs in this book were learned by the authors in the traditional way: from the singing or playing of others, who had in turn learned these songs from other singers or musicians. Sometimes individual performers have claimed the copyright of their versions or arrangements of old songs or tunes.

We give here, or in the text, some of what we know about who first made or kept alive the original songs or tunes. However, please remember that these songs and tunes have often changed greatly, and continue to live, in the hands or mouths of performers.

Coulter's Candy is an old song which was made widely popular when printed by Norman Buchan in a newspaper column and in his book *101 Scottish Songs*. Various people have rewritten verses or made new ones for this song.
Today is Hogmanay was learned by Ewan McVicar from his parents.
Wee Gallus Bloke was recorded from Josh Shaw of Glasgow.
The Bonnie Ship The Diamond – there are several versions of this song, but it seems The Diamond sailed from Aberdeen, not Peterhead, and that the captain's name was Gibbons.
The Blantyre Explosion – there are two tunes in use for this song and we use the simpler one.
McGinty's Meal and Ale was written by G S Morris and Willy Kemp.
The Gypsy Laddies – hundreds of versions of this ballad have been recorded or noted down all over the world.
Corriechoilles and *Bonnie Ann* were composed by Pipe Major W Ross.
The Yesterman's Hand and *The Old Man's Answer* were composed by Brian McNeill.
Skye Boat Song was written by Sir Harold Boulton.
The Bloody Fields of Flanders was written by John McLellan.

You will find other versions of many of the songs in the eight volumes of *The Greig-Duncan Folk Song Collection*, in various books by Norman Buchan, Sheila Douglas, Ewan MacColl and Peggy Seeger, and in collections of the works of Robert Burns.

The largest, most important collection of traditional Scottish song and instrumental music is held in the archives of the School of Scottish Studies, University of Edinburgh, 27 George Square, Edinburgh EH8 9LD. This book and CD could not have been made without the support, advice and encouragement of the School's director, Dr Margaret Mackay, and other staff members.

STORIES

Giant Fitba, *The Hungry Cabin Boy*, *The Worser* and *David Down The Pit* were all written by Ewan McVicar. All the other stories have been rewritten by Ewan McVicar. You may hear versions of some of them from other storytellers and find them in collections of Scottish traditional tales.

RECORDINGS

All the recordings labelled 'CDTRAX' on page 60 are issued by Greentrax Recordings Ltd of Cockenzie, East Lothian. The Greentrax 'Scottish Tradition' series of recordings are chosen and prepared from the sound archive of the School of Scottish Studies.
The Lea Rig, performed by Julia Lane of the group Castlebay, from Maine, USA, is from the group's album *Tapestry II In A Garden Green*, CMT2D, © Castlebay 2000.

FURTHER READING, LISTENING AND CONTACTS

BOOKS ABOUT SCOTTISH SONG AND MUSIC

The Democratic Muse: folk music revival in Scotland by Ailie Munro (with a chapter by Morag MacLeod on Folk Revival in Gaelic Song), published by Scottish Cultural Press, 1996.

Rantin' Pipe and Tremblin' String: a history of Scottish dance music by George S Emmerson, published by J M Dent & Sons, 1971.

Scotland's Music by John Purser, published by Mainstream Publishing, 1992.

Scottish Traditional Music by Nicola Wood, published by Chambers, 1991.

The Traditional and National Music of Scotland by Francis Collinson, published by Routledge & Kegan Paul, 1966.

Traditional Music in Scotland, Education Information Advocacy, a report published by the Scottish Arts Council, 1999

BOOKS WITH SCOTTISH SONGS AND TUNES

Children's songs

Golden City by J T R Ritchie, published by Mercat Press, 1999.

Classic Children's Games from Scotland by Kendric Ross, published by Scottish Children's Press, 1996.

Sangs, Reels and High Jinks, a Teachers' Pack published by Dumfries and Galloway Arts Association, 1999.

Collections of songs

The Scottish Folksinger edited by Norman Buchan and Peter Hall, published by Collins, 1974.

Come Gie's a Sang: 73 traditional Scottish songs edited by Sheila Douglas with Jo Miller, published by The Hardie Press, 1995.

The Sang's The Thing edited by Sheila Douglas (includes interviews with singers), published by Polygon, 1992.

Scottish Ballads edited by Emily Lyle, published by Canongate, 1994.

One Singer One Song: songs of Glasgow folk by Ewan McVicar, published by Glasgow City Libraries, 1990.

Scottish Songs and Ballads edited by Nancy Marshall, published by Chambers, 1990.

Ord's Bothy Songs and Ballads by John Ord, published by John Donald, 1990.

Ossian Publications have produced a fine selection of songbooks, including three volumes of *Traditional Folksongs & Ballads of Scotland, The Scottish Songs of Robert Burns* and *The Words of 100 Scots Songs and Ballads.*

The eight volumes of *The Greig-Duncan Folk Song Collection* published by Mercat Press (1981-2001) have thousands of texts and tunes of songs collected around 100 years ago in north-east Scotland, discussion of the songs, and detail of the singers.

Collections of Instrumental Tunes

An Fhideag Airgid: A Whistle Tutor for Highland Music by Davey Garrett, published by TM & CS, 1994.

Scottish Fiddle Music in the 18th Century: a music collection and historical study by David Johnson, published by Mercat Press, 1997.

The Scots Fiddle: tunes, tales and traditions by J Murray Neil, published by Neil Wilson Publishing, 1999.

Taigh na Teud (see page 63 for website), based on the Isle of Skye, produce tune books for fiddle, harp, piano, guitar, accordion and bagpipes. See particularly their *Ceol na Fidhle* series and their *Ceilidh Collections* for fiddle.

BOOKS ABOUT SCOTS WORDS

Scots School Dictionary edited by Iseabail Macleod and Pauline Cairns, published by Polygon, 1999.

Scots Thesaurus edited by Iseabail Macleod et al, published by Polygon, 1999.

The Concise Scots Dictionary edited by Mairi Robinson, published by Polygon, 1999.

The Scots Dialect Dictionary by Alexander Warrack, published by Chambers, 1987.

BOOKS WITH SCOTTISH STORIES

The Well At The World's End by Norah and William Montgomerie, published by Bodley Head, 1975.

Fireside Tales of the Traveller Children and *The Broonie, Silkies and Fairies* by Duncan Williamson, published by Canongate, 1983 and 1993.

Duncan and Linda Williamson have written a number of other books of traditional Scottish stories, all published by Canongate.

Scottish Traditional Tales edited by Alan Bruford and Donald A MacDonald, published by Polygon, 1994.

The Penguin Book of Scottish Folktales edited by Neil Philip, published by Penguin, 1995.

RECORDINGS OF SCOTTISH SONG AND MUSIC

The 'Scottish Tradition' series, issued by Greentrax with the School of Scottish Studies, is full of gems from our tradition and culture. We would particularly recommend *The Muckle Sangs*, Scottish Tradition 5, CDTRAX 9005, on which are twenty-seven sung versions of ballads, and *Music from the Western Isles: an introduction to the Gaelic music of Scotland*, Scottish Tradition 2, CDTRAX 9002, which has a wonderful range of Gaelic song types. *Bothy Ballads: music from the North-East*, Scottish Tradition 1, CDTRAX 9001, is also an excellent collection of songs and music.

Greentrax specialises in Scottish music, old and new. To get their catalogue, contact Greentrax Recordings Ltd, Cockenzie Business Centre, Edinburgh Road, Cockenzie, East Lothian EH32 0HL, tel. 01875 814155. There are several other record labels who issue recordings of Scottish music. Try Culburnie, Dunkeld, Linn, Springthyme, Temple and Living Tradition.

RADIO PROGRAMMES on BBC Radio Scotland

Travelling Folk, Thursday evenings, 7pm to 10pm

Iain Anderson, weekday afternoons, 2pm to 4pm

MAGAZINES

Living Tradition, a bi-monthly magazine available from newsagents or from PO Box 1026, Kilmarnock KA2 0LG.

Songs, tunes, stories and interviews from the archives of the School of Scottish Studies are issued in their publication *Tocher*, available on subscription from the School of Scottish Studies.

WEBSITES

www.folkfax.net A useful database of tunes, lyrics and information.

www.folkmusic.net Living Tradition Magazine, published in Scotland.

www.mudcat.org Use this site to access the Digital Tradition Folksong Database of lyrics and tunes.

www.musicscotland.com For purchase of CDs, and to listen to MP3 music samples.

www.pearl.arts.ed.ac.uk The School of Scottish Studies' PEARL site, with music and stories from the magazine *Tocher*.

www.scotlandsmusic.com For purchase of books and CDs (Taigh na Teud series).

www.storytellingcentre.org.uk The site of the Scottish Storytelling Centre.

www.tmsa.demon.co.uk/tmsa/home/tmsa.html The site of the Traditional Music and Song Association of Scotland.

members.jings.com/~traditional To contact the authors of this book with a query or to send them a new song or tune.

ORGANISATIONS IN SCOTLAND

Feisean Nan Gàidheal (The National Association of Gaelic Arts Youth Tuition Festivals), Nicolson House, Somerled Square, Portree, Isle of Skye IV51 9EJ, tel. 01478 613355.

Proiseact Nan Ealan (National Gaelic Arts Project), 10 Shell St, Stornoway, Isle of Lewis HS1 2EA, tel. 01851 704493/703440.

The Piping Centre, 30-34 McPhater Street, Glasgow G4 0HW, tel. 0141 353 0220.

Scottish Storytelling Centre, The Netherbow, 43-45 High Street, Edinburgh EH1 1SR, tel. 0131 556 9579/2647.

Scottish Music Information Centre, 1 Bowmont Gardens, Glasgow G12 9LR, tel. 0141 334 6393.

The School of Scottish Studies, University of Edinburgh, 27 George Square, Edinburgh EH8 9LD, tel. 0131 650 4167.

The Scottish Traditions of Dance Trust, 54 Blackfriars Street, Edinburgh EH1 1NE, tel. 0131 558 8737.

The Traditional Music and Song Association of Scotland, 95-97 St Leonard's St, Edinburgh EH8 9QY, tel. 0131 667 5587.

INDEX OF SONGS, TUNES, TOPICS AND STORIES

Entries given in italics are songs or tunes which include printed music in this book. Entries given in bold are stories.